educating the public library user

compiled and edited
by
john lubans, jr.

american
library
association
chicago
1983

R025.56

Educating...

Designed by Vladimir Reichl

Text composed by Caron Communications
in Roman P.S. and Titan on a Xerox
800 Word Processor. Display type,
Quorum, composed by Pearson Typographers

Printed on 50-pound Glatfelter,
a pH-neutral stock, and bound
in Tuscan cover stock by
Malloy Lithographing, Inc.

Library of Congress Cataloging in Publication Data
Main entry under title:

Educating the ·public library user.

Bibliography: p.
1. Library orientation--Addresses, essays,
lectures. 2. Libraries and readers--Addresses,
essays, lectures. 3. Public libraries--Addresses,
essays, lectures. I. Lubans, John.
Z711.2.E36 1983   025.5'6   83-11762
ISBN 0-8389-0382-7

MLK

contents

Contents

preface

This book results from the growing awareness that people do not know how to use a library, any type of library, and that something needs to be done. This anthology of original papers explores what that something might be and how to bring about changes. If this book makes the reader think and discuss why or why not the public library should be involved and promotes an expanded awareness of instruction in the use of libraries, it will have achieved its mission.

The expected audience is, of course, the public librarian; however, as the book points out, user education occurs in all types of libraries and so the nonpublic librarian will also benefit from a better understanding of what happens in this regard in the public library. After all, the same users patronize all types of libraries. In order for the public to progressively gain an appreciation for information-finding and using skills, all types of librarians will need to become involved in attempting such a change.

The library school instructor and student may also see relevance in this volume to classes on public services librarianship, reference service, and outreach programming.

Another reader group, perhaps the most reluctant and yet the most important, is represented by the teacher who expects his or her students to use the public library. As several of the contributors suggest, the key to improved use is held by the teachers--without their involvement and support little improvement will be seen. This volume, at the least, shows the willingness of public librarians to work with the teacher towards the same goal: educated people.

I wish to thank the contributors for their fine work and their willingness, in spite of other obligations, to share their ideas with the profession. Herbert Bloom, Senior Editor at ALA, has also, through insightful questions, contributed suggestions and direction for this volume. His help is appreciated. And lastly, a sigh of relief for my one-year-old daughter Mara, who, while teething, spared the manuscripts, preferring to gnaw hardbound volumes to those yet in the making.

John Lubans, Jr.

introduction

Educating the Public Library User describes the instruction of public library users in its distinct aspects. It is divided into several parts to illustrate these aspects. The first chapter is a general introductory essay by John Lubans, Jr., on the subject of user education in the public library. It raises questions about the location of the public library in education, what instructional links can be forged between public and other libraries, and gives reasons for user education.

Next, Peggy Sullivan, Ilene Nelson, and Anne Hyland, in individual chapters, write about the state of the art from their respective viewpoints. Ilene Nelson examines what the public library should be doing; Peggy Sullivan gives us an administrative viewpoint of user education; and Anne Hyland provides a thorough discussion of the school library--what it does in user education, how this interacts with the public library, and to a certain extent what the public library can expect of its school-age users.

The adult user of the public library is the focus of two chapters. Sheila Dale of Britain's Open University brings to light the operation of that institution in its broadcasting of education programs to thousands of university level students. It is relevant to this volume in that the English public library works hand-in-glove with the Open University in providing information resources to students for their continuing education. The recent (1981) multimillion dollar grant to emulate the Open University concept here in the United States heightens this relevancy. The adult lifelong learner, as viewed by John Shirk, represents a large "market" for the public library. His "Library Learning Climate Inventory" is one approach to gaining an appreciation of this user group and for promoting programs to reach this largely untapped market.

Since some readers will wish to pursue a user education program, the next area discussed by John Lubans, Jr., is planning and implementing. Emphasis is placed on standard planning processes along with examples drawn from the literature of academic and school library instruction. The evaluation aspect is stressed.

Case studies make up a major division of this volume. They are a selection of applications in small and large libraries for children and adults from here and abroad. The reader should run across numerous ideas for adaptation and learn to detour around the pitfalls from others' trials and errors. The practical approach, taken by all of the authors, is augmented by their critical remarks on how well their program is doing, how it could be improved (internally and externally) and where their program fits in the overall concept of educating the public library user. Frank Smith and Judy Pate, Lee White, and Margaret Hendley describe their adult user education programs and Ann Scarpellino and David Miller give us insights into their programs for children and young adults.

A bibliography on the topic culled from a variety of sources is appended. It and the readings suggested in the contributed chapters should give readers a wide variety of general and specialized discussion on the topic.

the role of the
public library in achieving
library literacy

This paper is theoretically based on the concept that user education programs inside and outside the public library are a feasible and resourceful way of improving both the image and the use of the public library and, in turn, of all libraries. The goal of this teaching effort, individually or in collaboration with other libraries, is to develop a population that can be termed library literate. Library literacy, or the ability to find and use information, is increasingly recognized as a vital component of the critical thinking or decision-making processes.

I have organized this chapter into three topical divisions: the user education movement and its meaning for the public library; an analysis of reasons for instruction in public library use; and, finally some intimations of change and suggested directions.

USER EDUCATION MOVEMENT

In other types of libraries, particularly the academic, user education could be termed a growth industry. While its roots in academia are traceable to the late 1800s, the last decade has shown an unprecedented burgeoning of both the literature and day-to-day library applications. Most representative of the maturation of this specialized interest is the recent formation of the Bibliographic Instruction Section (BIS) of the Association of College and Research Libraries (ACRL), a division of the American Library Association (ALA). BIS, devoted entirely to user education in academic libraries, is one of the largest and most active sections within ACRL with multiple committees, publications, and programs.

A stranger to the scene would quickly (and accurately) gain the impression of academic librarian predominance in publications on instruction and conferences on the topic. However, while not so prolific in broadcasting their achievements, the school librarian (both grammar and high school) may in fact instruct more students using a broader base of teaching methods than do counterparts in academia.

1

Public libraries, along with special libraries, are least heard from. That they do offer user education programs at all levels can be verified by perusing this book, especially the case studies and the bibliography. Not dissimilar to much of the instruction offered in other libraries in its variety and uncertainty of impact, it can be characterized as developmental. Whether public libraries should be involved in user education is a moot question. Instead, questions need to be raised about the magnitude of the public library's role in user education; what techniques can be created or adapted from other libraries; and, what collaborations might be formed to enhance the impact of user education efforts in all types of libraries.

Recognizing the interdisciplinary trend there is the eight-hundred member Library Instruction Round Table (LIRT) of ALA, which provides a focus on issues of user instruction in all types of libraries. Some measure of LIRT's commitment to user education across the spectrum of interests is found in its inaugural program in 1978, "The Public Library: Teaching the User" at the ALA conference in Chicago. LIRT's 1981 offering explored instructional linkages among public, school, college, and community college libraries. Its emphasis was on the articulation of services in different types of libraries. It concluded with the recognition that a broader library pattern on the part of learners must be the aim of library instruction.

At the state level, attention is beginning to shift from a single type of library user education to consideration of the influences of various libraries on user skills. For example, the South Carolina Library Association in the fall of 1980 pointedly asked "Does the Left Hand Know What the Right Hand Is Doing?" about interactions among public, school and academic library user education programs.

On the international scene, the interdisciplinary trend is also visible. The second international conference on user education in Oxford, England, in 1981 featured discussion about all types of libraries, whereas the first conference (1979) dealt only with academic issues. Of interest is a letter produced by the conferees aimed at the British Library Association (LA). It proposed, as published in the October 1981 issues of Infuse, that the LA either designate a headquarters staff member to coordinate development in public library user education in England or that an ad hoc committee explore this development. More importantly, there was the additional recommendation that the LA collaborate in this regard with ALA's Public Information Office, and publishers, associations, and other agencies concerned with library use.

Two anthologies of original writings, one published in 1974 and the other in 1978, serve as a forum for programs in all libraries. These are Educating the Library User and Progress in Educating the Library User. A reading of these provides practical and theoretical insights into user education programs in all types of libraries. Both volumes emphasize the need for improved relationships among libraries across the traditional boundaries.

2

So, we say with some certainty that user education exists in all types of libraries. Unfortunately there are few if any links among these libraries concerning what is taught or how it is taught or to what end it is taught. Since libraries share the same user, so to speak, these gaps result in an all too prevalent redundancy and uncertainty of value in our efforts. While programs exist in each type of library, the connecting links or channels for sharing programs, ideas, and energy between the libraries do not.

By forging the links between programs we may achieve a learning and teaching continuum for library literacy. The public library is deliberately central to this goal. If one imagines what libraries are used during a user's life span, the conclusion is that it is largely the public library. It would seem then of importance for the public library to strive for a continuum in user education to match the continuum of use. This is the spirit in which the council of the American Library Association specifically stated " . . . all libraries [should] include instruction in the use of libraries as one of the primary goals of service."[1] The full policy statement is given in the appendix.

REASONS FOR INSTRUCTION IN PUBLIC LIBRARY USE

While many librarians will support library instruction on its face value alone, there are a number of unanswered questions that make it difficult to gain support from those who are in administrative positions; their skepticism is usually based on several popular but ill-founded notions. Arguments are often presented as to why public libraries and user education may be incompatible.

Before restating these arguments, let us spotlight the point when someone needs to know something. It is here that not knowing how to use a library is most felt--both by the would-be user and the library that may not be used. What are the general ramifications of this for libraries and how does user education fit in?

The three-part figure 1 is a snapshot of what occurs when someone, a potential library user, has an information need. This is not necessarily inside the library; rather it typifies the influences and outcomes one finds surrounding and emerging from a "simple" question: be it advice on a purchase, a career change, or research for a school project.

At "A" in our illustration the user is seen with a particular need for information. The satellites surrounding the user show that the user and his or her inquiry do not exist in a vacuum. Rather the user's environment is full of competing influences. Those illustrated all play major roles--in fact some may be the source of the question, e.g., it may be a job-related problem. Socioeconomic variables such as level of income, age, and ethnicity have been shown as influences on user behavior in the information-seeking process. Education probably has great impact on what steps will be taken in search of an answer. As a subvariable, very likely, the user's prior exposure to libraries and their use can have

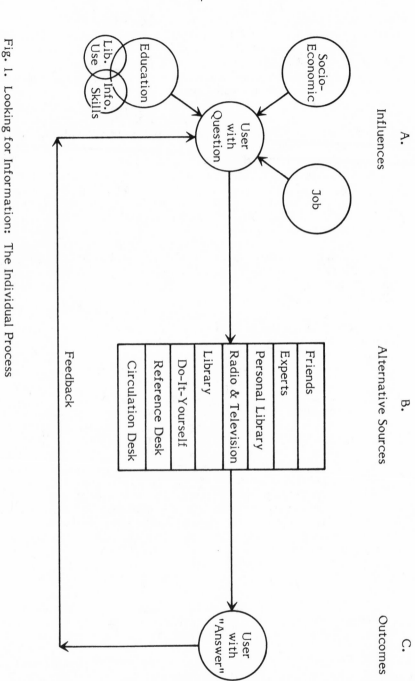

A. Influences

B. Alternative Sources

C. Outcomes

Socio-Economic

Education

Lib. Use Info. Use Skills

User with Question

Job

Friends

Experts

Personal Library

Radio & Television

Library

Do-It-Yourself

Reference Desk

Circulation Desk

User with "Answer"

Feedback

Fig. 1. Looking for Information: The Individual Process

even more bearing on the information trail taken. Education that is not "library-based" is unlikely to produce lifelong users of libraries. Jo Anne Nordling, speaking about high school students, concludes:

> It is regrettable, but true, that many of the young people who avoid the high school library as though it were the plague are ever after uncomfortable around any library. For the rest of their lives they pass up the one . . . constantly expanding information source available to them.[2]

"B" in figure 1 suggests some of the choices available to the information seeker. As the list reveals, the library is but one source where the user can get help. It is infrequently the first choice, and may often not be considered at all by information seekers working through sources they think will have the answer. Library use (or nonuse) studies confirm this unsettling fact about all libraries. A recent national Gallup poll found nonuse at around 50 percent among people above 18 years of age.[3] A study in New Orleans determined nonuse was around 60 percent for people 12 years or older.[4] Nonuse does not seem to be going away on its own volition. Library public relations programs that equate library use with knowing about a library fail to recognize the vast difference between the two.

If the individual at point "B" chooses the library as a source there are several ways to proceed. These include "do it yourself," ask for help at the information desk (if there is one) either in person or by telephone, or ask someone that works in the library, e.g., at the circulation desk. Beyond the rawest quantities and some theoretical writing we know little about the user's interaction with the library. The information-seeking and using process and the quality of the result are largely unknown. Some recent studies that examine the situations are a bit pessimistic about what one may find individually or how helpful the reference or circulation points may be.[5] Misuse, unlike nonuse, is a profound mystery. At the visceral level, many librarians see misuse as epidemic. Martin expresses this view when, writing of the alleged need for more books to support student reading, he pointed out that "a significant part of the problem is that young people do not locate what is actually available."[6]

Of course misuse is not limited to libraries. We know practically nothing about the quality of the information-gaining process if one opts to use a nonlibrary source. Finding the best answer is not an easy matter--it is possible that, the more discerning the information use skills one has, the higher the quality of the outcome will be. In response to this assumption, point-of-use instruction has been promoted in academic libraries. By allowing, usually through mechanical means, users to sharpen their skills at the time they need them, such programs seek to aid the user in vending his or her way through the information maze. These are generally quick, to the point, and highly specialized explanations. Examples include a two-minute silent film loop on use of a magazine index and a ten-minute slide tape introduction to the card catalog. The theory behind point-of-use instruction is that the user does need to know but does not have the time or interest to devote an hour or more to such esoterics as search strategy or the differences between general encyclopedias and subject encyclopedias.

Whether or not the user has gotten an answer he or she concludes the search upon arrival at point "C" in figure 1. If the user believes the process has been successful he or she will probably remember it and retrace the path when another inquiry comes up. If the user has been frustrated or misled, whether through self- or another's ignorance, the feedback will tend to be negative. If one thinks the library has failed, he or she will probably not use it again, choosing instead a nonlibrary source. The cyclical aspect of this process is observable. Interrupting or changing the cycle of nonuse and misuse, no mean undertaking, is of course a large part of the user education effort.

"The Jury Is Still Out"

A particularly frequent criticism heard against user education is that there is no scientific evidence in support of the positive claims made by user education advocates. The need to "prove" the value of new programs is shared by most service agencies. Much of what we traditionally do in libraries is not based on quantitative analyses; rather we apply intuition and professional judgment, a strong dose of incremental decision making and continue to fund programs from year to year--as do most, if not all, organizations be they profit or non-profit.

Admittedly the scientific record is spotty; yet there is a growing body of evaluation literature that suggests user education programs do have a substantial impact.[7] Evaluation of academic library programs and long-range effects are showing results. Controlled experiments have demonstrated that students with instruction use the library more and at higher levels than students not instructed. One public library program for inner-city students concludes that, as a result of the program, borrower registration doubled, circulation went up five percent, and professional services increased by 32 percent.[8]

A great deal more needs to be done in establishing a solid research base. The research record is indicating an increased interest in moving beyond intuition to gaining evidence to back up the case for user education.

"Library Use Is Easy"

One of the major stumbling blocks in the user education movement is the myth that library use is, or should be, a simple task. This belief is endorsed by more than a few librarians and underlies student and teacher attitudes toward libraries. The apotheosis of this view was recently found in a well-meaning national advertisement on library use where James Michener, the famed novelist, advised us about the card catalog: "Learn to use it. It's easy."[9]

In our zeal to convince people about the importance of libraries we may have overstressed the idea that finding and using information is a skill easily acquired; almost as if upon entering the library the answer to one's question will be waiting. Perhaps, we've been brainwashed by our own propaganda.

Most basic skills take time to acquire. Few of us became literate overnight nor did we master the multiplication of fractions at one sitting. It is the same with finding information.

The view that libraries are easy to use may account for what can only be termed our suspension of disbelief of the fact that people have a hard time using libraries. This is most evident in programs that stress the importance and value of reading but fail to equip the individual with the wherewithal to find the books to read.

Aiding and abetting the "it's easy" view is the encroaching computer. Somehow the machine is to facilitate use of the card catalog. How it is to do this is not explained. Perhaps the computer has the potential (it certainly has more appeal than the traditional card catalog), but since it is modeled on manual systems, are not the inherent difficulties of use still there? Until we load, in our thesaurus, the L.C. List of Subject Headings (and make its cross references easy to use), the user will still find the subject approach hard going. Will corporate entries be any less a seemingly insurmountable hurdle?

"Who Cares?"

Library instruction librarians can take heart. It isn't just librarians who are demanding that something be done. In answer to what should be done to improve and increase library use, several state governor's conferences on libraries (all with a lay person majority) pointed to needed improvements in information skills. Epitomizing the resolutions passed in other states such as Michigan and Virginia is that from Connecticut:

> Be it resolved that the State Department of Education mandate a program of instruction in the use of library resources . . . to enable children to become independent learners and users of libraries in their adult years, and that public and academic libraries offer user programs to develop their library skills.[10] (emphasis added)

These opinions, representing a variety of views and interests, came together in the 1979 White House Conference. The result, similar to the governor conferences, was the resolution on "public awareness" which calls for an "aggressive, comprehensive nationwide . . . campaign" by all types of libraries. The goal is to endow citizens with library "skills and aptitudes necessary to function and take advantage of (library) services. . . ."[11]

7

"Let George Do It"

One should expect, and reasonably so, that skills learned in one library should transfer effectively to another type of library. After all, the same tools, varying in numbers, exist in most libraries: indexes for books and magazines; dictionaries and encyclopedias, biographical directories, handbooks, guides, etc., are found in all libraries. However, one of the most puzzling concerns in user education today is the apparent nontransfer of library skills. The byword at college level is to assume the user knows little or nothing about library use. The same situation presents itself in the public library. Martin found in 1963 that "if instruction in resource skill is a proper secondary school objective it can only be observed that it is an objective that is not achieved."[12] DeSomogyi reaffirmed this view in 1975 and compounded it by adding that "instruction in library skills should figure prominently in the syllabus, but, in the face of faculty indifference, students cannot be expected to take it seriously."[13]

In spite of what might be called ideal conditions (captive audiences, classroom project requiring library use) user education programs have yet to see consistent and long-term application of their teachings by users. At one time librarians were prone to blame this circumstance on their "amateurish" attempts at teaching or that their instruction, e.g., about the card catalog, was in fact "deadening." Now there is the conviction that without any change in the curriculum on the role of the library, it will continue to be used on an all too infrequent basis. This conclusion is reached by comparing the effectiveness of teaching and learning given the central or peripheral role of the library in a course of study. Apparently the irregular exercise of these skills leads to their atrophy. Hence the redundancy and remedial aspect of much of the instruction offered in libraries. It is then fallacious to believe that users come endowed with these skills.

"We Do It All for You"

When I ask a public librarian about instructing users, a common response is that there is no need because public libraries are different. They are different in that users receive complete answers regardless of the frivolity or complexity of the question. Some libraries do strive to achieve this ideal, at least with some of their users, but even the most casual observer will quickly doubt the success of this panoptic service mission.

One recent study gives us some insights as to how effective reference service is and how thorough it is in covering the needs of users.[14] Childers undertook an unobtrusive analysis of 50 public libraries in a large system near a major metropolitan area. Eleven hundred carefully framed questions were asked by researchers and library responses were analyzed closely.

The results:
Nearly half the questions were rejected or the questioner was referred to another library.[15]

Of the 625 questions that were answered, 84 percent of the answers were correct or mostly correct.

Sixteen percent of the 625 questions received wrong or mostly wrong answers.

These results suggest the user (or consumer) of libraries needs to be more skillful and discriminating in information use than at present.

Another area looked at by this study was that of "doing it yourself" as one way of gaining an answer to the question after asking for help at the information desk. Childers made 502 observations along this line and found far from "full service" being provided. Instead, as one would realistically expect, many users were encouraged to help themselves to the information resources. However the nagging question remains: were the users able to search out the answer on their own? Sixteen percent of the users were referred to the reference tools and accompanied by the librarian (whose presence should assure effective use of the tool). However, 18 percent were sent off unaccompanied to use a particular reference work. This 18 percent, when coupled with another 26 percent that were directed to "browse" alone for the answer, is a large group in this one study, that is either presumed to have adequate information-seeking skills or for whom serendipity is invoked because the staff does not have the time to help.

The very concept of doing it all for the user, even if not fully implemented, may be a harmful one. Aside from the hit and miss nature of the theory in practice, there is the sensible sounding criticism that our doing it all may backfire. It may lead to an overreliance on outside help that impedes the user's growth toward independent problem solving.

INTIMATIONS OF CHANGE IN USER EDUCATION

Where then to start? The emerging trends in other libraries may be worth noting and adapting. One assumes that since the trends and shifts in emphasis are based on actual successes and failures we stand to gain considerable insights. A look at the academic and school library reveals one major change: a movement toward instruction about the process of information seeking and using, away from that which stresses product, e.g., memorization of specific reference tools in which to find information. Process instruction relies on library awareness across the curriculum rather than its being pigeonholed in a single project or discipline. As such, this is a major change effort since both education and society at large are involved in changing how people are taught and in improving the role that information serves in society.[16]

Concurrent with other efforts to bring home the importance of effective information finding and using skills is the resurgent emphasis on critical thinking.[17] The process has been defined as the "ability to

9

grasp significant relationships from a mass of materials."[18] The library's role in critical thinking is a fundamental and vital one. It is in the library that the person has the opportunity "to inform oneself; i.e., to research a topic in a resourceful and creative fashion," so that the process of critical thought can be helped along.[19] The library needs to stress in its user education programs the how of finding out about something besides the standard solution of telling people about the tools in a particular subject field. This will involve elaboration on strategies of information seeking with attention to evaluation of the information found.

The depth of involvement remains a yet-to-be established standard. It will, no doubt, relate to the benefits gained from involvement. The case studies in this volume suggest directions and ideas for emulation. Other opportunities might include experimentation with small groups such as new citizens or the handicapped. Lowell Martin's conclusions, while for a specific case, may be of value because they are based on a thorough analysis of information needs of students. His report is not guesswork but rather a result of thousands of questionnaires and interviews.[20] The structure he proposes would take us beyond theory to application. His objective is getting full return from present resources. To achieve this he proposes: improved cooperation between the schools and the public library; the creation of a new position--the Student-Teacher Librarian; a teaching approach to student library service in both school and public libraries; and, a systematic orientation to resources when students come to prepare papers in depth. The new position is to be the change agent in bringing this about. Mindful of the realities, Martin sees the need for cooperative actions among the top levels of both the school and the library.

Unlike Martin's plan, the White House Conference recommendations do not suggest a structure for or methods of presenting user education.[21] At most, they are open qualitative goals toward which we are to strive, similar to an interpretation of the recent Gallup poll on library use, "Libraries must make it easier for less educated users to get information and they must use more publicity to encourage and increase use," but the how is not provided.[22] A valid concern is that these called-for efforts will not go beyond a stepped-up public relations campaign. If this is the case, our efforts will fail to address the underlying issues of library use. It bears saying again, knowing about a library is different from knowing how to use it.

The ubiquitous fiscal problems facing libraries do have a good aspect. The fiscal crunch may necessitate our looking inward for solutions to the pervasive conditions of nonuse and misuse (which in no small way have led us to the current impasse). High priced technology has yet to provide an answer in this area; user education has been shown able to make changes. If academic librarians are any indicators, user education is a grass roots activity absorbed by existing staff. It has been, until quite recently, a self-assumed, extra responsibility usually in the public services sector. The collegial nature of academic libraries may be one reason for the rapid growth of academic user education. In the public library setting it may be that strong advocacy of the top administration in the hierarchy will be the sine qua non in the chance of success for any program.

Furthermore, the need for formal and high level contact with other types of libraries, school administrators, boards of education, and teacher groups would make this a role for the key person in the library administration, in other words, the director of the library. Once links are forged it may be possible to delegate these responsibilities to someone like Martin's Student-Teacher Librarian.

Finally, it is hoped that the public library will, as a part of its instruction, expand its present programs and give its support to the library literacy cause. With all libraries examining the issues and learning from each other, we may be able to accomplish change in how libraries are perceived and used. The concerted effort of all libraries offers a better chance in influencing educational agencies than does that of any single type of library to move libraries from the periphery of education to its center.

Appendix

POLICY STATEMENT:
INSTRUCTION IN THE USE OF LIBRARIES

Utilization of information is basic to virtually every aspect of daily living in a democratic society, whether in the formal pursuit of educational goals or in independent judgment and decision making. In our post-industrial, increasingly complex society, the need for information daily becomes greater.

Libraries are a major source of information; however, their effective use requires an understanding of how information is organized and how individuals can retrieve that information. Many individuals have an inadequate understanding of how to determine the type of information needed, locate the appropriate information, and use it to their best advantage.

Instruction in the use of libraries should begin during childhood years and continue as a goal of the formal information retrieval essential to sustain lifelong professional and personal growth.

It is essential that libraries of all types accept the responsibility of providing people with opportunities to understand the organization of information. The responsibility of educating users in successful information location demands the same administrative, funding, and staffing support as do more traditional library programs.

The American Library Association encourages all libraries to include instruction in the use of libraries as one of the primary goals of service.

1979-80 ALA COUNCIL
DOCUMENT #45

11

NOTES

1. "Policy Statement: Instruction in the Use of Libraries," 1979-80 ALA Council Document no. 45 (Chicago: American Library Assn., 1980, mimeographed).

2. Jo Anne Nordling, Dear Faculty (Framingham, Mass.: Faxon, 1976), p.150.

3. "ALA Ponders Implications of Views on Libraries in New Gallup Survey," American Libraries 9 (November 1978):572.

4. Elizabeth Rountree, "Users and Nonusers Disclose Their Needs," American Libraries 10 (September 1979):468.

5. An example is Thomas Childers, The Effectiveness of Information Service in Public Libraries: Suffolk County; Final Report (Philadelphia: Drexel Univ., School of Library and Information Science, 1978).

6. Lowell A. Martin, Students and the Pratt Library: Challenge and Opportunity, Deiches Fund Studies of Public Library Service, no. 1 (Baltimore, Md.: Enoch Pratt Free Library, 1963).

7. In a paper for the Oxford, England, Second International Conference on User Education in July 1981, I reviewed a part of the evaluation literature and concluded that instructional programs have been shown quantitatively to influence and improve library use.

8. "Quadrus Promotes Libraries for Inner-City Children," American Libraries 12 (January 1981):46.

9. James A. Michener, "How to Use a Library," Psychology Today 14 (October 1980):61-62.

10. As reported in LOEX News 6 (March 1979):3.

11. "White House Conference, U.S.A.," Infuse 4 (April 1980):5-7.

12. Martin, Students and the Pratt Library, p.44.

13. Aileen DeSomogyi, "Library Skills: Now or Never," School Library Journal 22 (November 1975):37.

14. Childers, Effectiveness of Information Service, p.16.

15. About half were of the "no answer/reject" type and an equal amount of "referrals."

16. For example, see Ann Irving, "Educating Users--Is There Really a New Approach?" in John Lubans, Jr., ed., "Library Literacy," RQ 20 (Fall 1980):11-14; and Anne M. Hyland, "Recent Directions in Educating the Library User: Elementary Schools," in John Lubans, Jr., ed., Progress in Educating the Library User (New York: Bowker, 1978), pp.29-44.

17. Rockefeller Foundation, The Humanities in America (Berkeley, Calif.: Univ. of California Pr., 1980).

18. Carolyn O. Leopold, School Libraries Worth Their Keep (Metuchen, N.J.: Scarecrow, 1972), p.28.

19. "The BAS Program" (Canton, N.Y.: St. Lawrence Univ., 1980), p.2.

20. Martin, Students and the Pratt Library. This 1963 study anticipates much of the concern addressed by this volume. Martin undertook a questionnaire and interview study of the Enoch Pratt Free Library in

Baltimore, Maryland, and its relationship to student reading. From the 9,000 questionnaires and nearly 2,000 interviews he formed a ten-point program to preserve the strength of the Pratt Library as a reading resource and "insure youth of one of the most important means of education." The program includes four phases: Preliminary Steps; Getting Full Return from Present Sources (i.e., user education); Expansion to Meet Student Needs; and Experimentation and Planning. It is the last phase that proposes three new positions, all titled Student-Teacher Librarian, which would "facilitate student services through existing channels." Their primary role would be to assure communication between the schools and the public library, teachers, and librarians.

21. "White House Conference, U.S.A.," pp.5-7.

22. "Who Didn't You Reach Today?" (a bibliography on marketing strategies for educating library nonusers) (New York: Library Instruction Round Table, 1980, mimeographed), p.3.

establishing
links
between
libraries

who's
responsible for
what skills?

ILENE NELSON

It is an undisputed fact that user education is a topic that has received much more visible consideration from school and academic librarians than it has from public librarians. This should not be interpreted as a lack of concern among public librarians for the ability of people to use libraries. It only signifies that the concept of user education is much more complex in the context of the public library than it is in either school or academic libraries and, consequently, has been more difficult to resolve. School and academic libraries have easily identified roles and a well-defined, homogeneous clientele while public libraries attempt to meet the recreational, educational, and informational needs of all the community's residents from their infancy through their old age.

Because of this broad purpose and vast potential audience, one of the most difficult tasks in public library service has always been the judicious distribution of time and money to provide the best service for the greatest number of people. In making these allocations of funds and human resources for user education programs, one consideration must be the access patrons have to other libraries. It seems logical that school and academic libraries with their well-defined goal of service to a particular institution and its constituents should accept major responsibility for the skills instruction of students, as they have. However, anyone who has ever been in a public library on a weekday evening or a Sunday afternoon knows that students don't use their institutional libraries exclusively. One article has even suggested that they use public libraries more than they use their school libraries.[1] The result too often is an unsuccessful effort by students to apply one set of use skills to several different libraries.

Currently, specificity is the byword of library instruction. The ideal school or academic bibliographic instruction program is based on measurable objectives and related whenever possible to actual course work. This philosophy is creditable; however, it does have disadvantages. Most seriously, it assumes single library use restricting the application of information-seeking skills to a single set of circumstances. All public librarians have had the experience of dealing with students who are trying to find the author-title section of a dictionary catalog, or of explaining that while a Dewey number might not look like an LC number it serves the same purpose, or of encouraging the use of a periodical index more appropriate than the Readers' Guide. In each situation the students are victims of their limited knowledge, thwarted in their efforts to apply information to the solution of a problem because their information-seeking skills are dependent upon a fixed pattern of organization. While a certain amount of specificity is necessary in school and academic instruction programs in order to insure relevance, some method needs to be found to instill general concepts regarding the organization and application of information in order to facilitate a transference of skills.

If any real progress is to be made in giving school and academic library skills instruction a broader applicability, librarians in every community must begin talking to each other. We must abandon parochial considerations of ourselves as school, public, or academic librarians and begin to regard our libraries not as separate institutions with independent goals, but as component collections in the community information network. Within this construct school, public, and academic librarians together will consider all of the library resources in the community available to students and then cooperate in teaching the skills necessary to use them. Depending upon each situation, this might require instructional visits by students and the school librarian to the public library, or the use of videotape, or a cooperative presentation by the academic librarian and the public librarian to acquaint college students with public library resources pertinent to a particular course area. In this way the emphasis is shifted from a narrow concept, using a particular library and its resources, to a broader concept having as its foundation a recognition of the student as a whole person with current roles and information needs as well as a potential and need for lifelong use of information. Students will feel as confident about using other libraries in the community as they do about using their own school or academic library. It will become just as important for students to know that all libraries have some method of listing their holdings as it is for them to be able to use a specific catalog format. The concept that periodical literature is accessible through a variety of indexes will be promoted as vigorously as is the skill to interpret an entry from any one index.

But most significantly, in this new construct of libraries as components in the community information network, greater consideration can be given to the affective element of library use, how people feel about libraries and librarians. Traditional library instruction programs seem to leave a subconscious impression that librarians teach students to use libraries in order to free themselves from requests for assistance. The number of persons who preface questions to librarians with "excuse me" or "I'm sorry" demonstrate that in some way we convey the idea that a lack of self-reliance in using a library is cause for guilt. Perhaps when the emphasis in instruction programs is creative use of information rather than a mechanical application of skills, the

18

librarian will be considered a facilitator in the information-seeking process and not a judge of library competence.

Judy Troup, librarian at the L. E. Gable Middle School in Spartanburg, South Carolina, has initiated a unique program that introduces her students to the idea of libraries as links in the information network. She has prepared several videotape presentations on public, academic, and special libraries in the community which she then shows to her students as part of a skills instruction program that also acquaints them with the variety of information options available in their community. It is this sort of program which should typify the cooperative nature of developing instruction programs. Our view is too narrow if we consider facility in the use of a single library as the ultimate goal of any skills instruction program.

If we regard skills instruction programs for students to be the responsibility of school and academic librarians, then adults are the primary audience for user education programs initiated by public librarians. And it is the adults' motivation for using public libraries which should determine the methods by which this education is imparted.

School and academic libraries are the experimentation or laboratory component in the educational process that complements the classroom component. Thus, the information-seeking process is an integral part of the student's general education. It is this concept of the essentiality of the ability to locate and evaluate information as a major objective of a student's education that is the underlying and motivating element in school and academic library instruction programs and, to a certain extent, is a determining factor in the relationship between school and academic librarians and the users of their libraries. In public library use, however, the process by which the product is obtained, whether it is a current best-seller, an analysis of stock performance, or instructions for pruning trees, is of very little importance to most users. It is of little importance, that is, except in the degree to which it impedes progress toward obtaining the information product. The relationship between the public librarian and the user is also shaped by this emphasis on product. The public librarian's main concern is to insure that users obtain what they have come to the library for, not to insist that they know how to do it. Customer satisfaction, then, the library users' perception that they have gotten what they want, is the goal of all interactions between public librarians and public library users. The skills, or process, are only significant as contributing to this end.

Because of the greater importance of product as a motivating factor in public library use, passive forms of user education become the most significant. The library environment itself is the most critical agent in the balance between success and failure in the information-seeking process. The responsibility is with the public librarian to guarantee that the library environment contributes to the user's success in obtaining the information product rather than hindering it. Think about the library you work in. Has there been a conscious effort to organize materials in a manner determined by the logic of use, or has the arrangement been haphazard or decided by the physical limitations or peculiarities of the building or for staff convenience?

Public libraries should be more like supermarkets. Almost without exception supermarkets are arranged with the produce up one outside wall, the meat across the back of the store, the dairy products on the other side wall, and everything else in the middle, typically identified by easily read signs suspended from the ceiling. The structure itself and the organization of the contents within it are purely functional, designed to merchandise the product. Now think of all the public libraries you have been in. A circulation desk usually located near the entrance is virtually the only consistent similarity. There is too much emphasis attached to the building and its aesthetic qualities when the first concern should be how well it permits the presentation of the product. A public library user will need far fewer skills to use a library if its structure and the manner in which the materials are arranged do not function as a barrier to use.

The use of signs is another passive form of user education that generally receives only minimal consideration in libraries. In other public places such as hospitals, stores, air terminals, or government buildings, a well-integrated sign system is most often the rule rather than the exception. Only in libraries, it seems, are signs a low-priority item, their importance as an essential component in the library's user education program either ignored or unrecognized.

Various types of printed materials constitute the most often used passive form of user education in public libraries. They may be booklists, guides to the library, descriptions of a particular service, or an explanation of the use of a specific resource. They may be distributed as a handout during a special program, left to be picked up at various service points, or be permanently on display as point-of-use instruction. Or they may be distributed in a variety of ways outside the library, depending upon their purpose. Any print format thoughtfully designed and placed in the hands of a user or a potential user can go a long way toward educating the public library user.

Perhaps because of the philosophy of skills instruction in school and academic libraries, it generally is not considered acceptable to include these passive formats in any serious discussion of library user education. The implication is that only formal programs of group instruction have any real validity. However, while this format may be the most effective approach in school and academic libraries, the more heterogeneous nature of public library users and their generally internal rather than external motivation for using the library reduce the potential for success of group instruction in public libraries. Two public library group instruction programs which have been reported in the literature demonstrate this. Ruth Newman has reported and described Denver Public Library's workshop series, "How to Use the Library," in which thirty persons attended the four-part program that was eventually expanded to five sessions. The program included a history of books, printing, and libraries, with an overview of the Denver Public Library, an explanation of the card catalog, an introduction to a selection of reference books, and a two-part tour of the library.[2] Another formal program of instruction in a public library has been reported by Amy Louise Frey and Saul Spiegel of the West Hartford Public Library, Connecticut. The West Hartford program originated as a series of six workshops devoted to the introduction of general reference tools and evolved to a ten-part series, eight of which dealt with resources in a particular subject with the other two sessions devoted to a discussion of the card catalog and periodical indexes and a library tour.[3]   The attendance at the sessions has averaged seven. Both the Denver program and the West Hartford program seem to have been well-planned, well-publicized, and well-received by the people who attended. In terms of each library's potential service audience, however, each has reached a relatively small number of people. This does not mean that this type of program has no place in public libraries. It does mean that formal group instruction can only be regarded as one of many aspects of an effective public library user education program. As has been discovered at West Hartford and other libraries, group instruction in public libraries may be most appropriate when designed to interpret library resources and services to an audience with a specific information need: workers who want to improve their job performance, consumers who want to save money, genealogists who want to trace their families, or investors who want to earn a profit. Once again, for most public library users the process by which information is obtained is of much less interest than is the information itself.

The most valuable method of instruction in almost any circumstances is done on a one-to-one basis. In this context the level of instruction is geared to the learner's capabilities and the information presented is tailored precisely to the question being considered. This form of instruction may on the surface seem an impossible goal in public libraries, but is it? If we begin to build our libraries so that the structure contributes to successful use, if we organize the materials within them strictly with the user in mind, if we insist on adequate signs, if we make the best use of point-of-use and other passive instructional formats, won't we eliminate the need for much of the assistance which we are now offering and free ourselves for more specific and complex instruction? Rather than being restricted to a hurried explanation of a single tool we will more often be able to offer individual library users guidance in the discovery, evaluation, and use of the full range of information sources that have applicability to an immediate information need. Relevant reference materials, books, magazine and newspaper articles, documents, vertical file items, audiovisuals, and referral to private and governmental agencies, people, and libraries in the information network are the best demonstration of the information-seeking process.

Virtually every public library practices at least some form of user education. The failure is that most often these user education programs have been accidental and incomplete. This state of affairs cannot continue. The growing rivalry for funding among publicly supported institutions as well as competition in information delivery

21

from developing services such as The Source, CompuServ, Knowledge Index, and BRS/After Dark, will require the realization by a majority of a community's residents of the practical value of public libraries. This realization will only come when patrons recognize the public library as a community information source and then use it successfully to obtain desired materials and information.

We live in a world of fast food, drive-in windows, and 24-hour service. This necessitates a recognition among public librarians that public libraries must accommodate the user. If we wish to see public libraries meet their full service potential in the community, we must do everything we can to streamline the information-seeking process to insure successful delivery of the information product. We must have buildings which facilitate use, we must organize our collections for accessibility, and we must creatively combine passive and active instructional formats to educate users for effective library use.

While our immediate concern is that people be skillful enough to use libraries successfully, the ultimate goal is to instill in the user a lifelong realization of the value of library use. The attainment of this goal requires that we accept the challenge of strengthening the bonds among libraries at the local level. The consequence of this increased cooperation will be comprehensive library service that fosters the level of information use that we seek to encourage.

NOTES

1. Joan F. Cooke and Janice Spallholz, "With Moon Goers in Mind," Bookmark 29 (October 1969):12-13.
2. Ruth T. Newman, "Instructing the Out-of-School Adult in Public Library Use," in John Lubans, Jr., ed., Educating the Library User (New York: Bowker, 1974).
3. Amy Louise Frey and Saul Spiegel, "Educating Adult Users in the Public Library," Library Journal 104 (15 April 1979):894-96.

BIBLIOGRAPHY

Anspaugh, Sheryl. "Public Libraries: Teaching the User?" In Progress in Educating the Library User, edited by John Lubans, Jr. New York: Bowker, 1978.

Davies, Ruth Ann. "Educating Library Users in the Senior High School." In Educating the Library User, edited by John Lubans, Jr. New York: Bowker, 1974.

Eberhart, W. Lyle. "A Closer Look: Gallup Survey of American Adults Assesses the Role of Libraries in America." American Libraries 7 (April 1976):206-9.

Hannigan, Margaret C. "Orientation of the Out-of-School Adult to the Use of Public Libraries." ALA Bulletin 61 (July-August 1967):829-30.

Hartmann, Jill S., and Robert R. Hartmann. "Inviting Design Helps the User." Wisconsin Library Bulletin 73 (July-August 1977):161-62.

Jeffrey, Penelope S. "Library Instruction for Young Adults in Public Libraries." In Educating the Library User, edited by John Lubans, Jr. New York: Bowker, 1974.

Lerner, Louis A. "Erasing Barriers to Knowledge: A National Program Proposed by the NCLIS." Wisconsin Library Bulletin 69 (November-December 1973):356-57.

"Mission Statement for Public Libraries." American Libraries 8 (December 1977):615-20.

Molz, Kathleen R. "The 'State of the Art' of Public Library Orientation." Maryland Libraries 34 (Winter 1968):10-17.

Parks, Lethene. "User-Oriented Service: The Librarian as Helper." Public Libraries 17 (Winter 1978):14-15.

Peck, Theodore P. "Reference Librarian Recast in a New Role." RQ 11 (Spring 1972):212-13.

Solon, Avis, and Lare Mischo. "Ways through the Library Maze." Wisconsin Library Bulletin 73 (July-August 1977):163-64.

Stick, Dorothy. "Public Library/School Library Cooperation Eyed in Iowa." Library Journal 103 (1 May 1978):923-24.

"The WHCLIS Resolutions." American Libraries 11 (January 1980):22-23.

Zweizig, Douglas, and Brenda Dervin. "Public Library Use, Users, Uses. . . ." In Advances in Librarianship, edited by Melvin J. Voigt and Michael H. Harris. New York: Academic, 1977.

an administrative view
of instruction
in the use
of public libraries

PEGGY SULLIVAN

Administration consists of making and implementing of decisions. Those decisions require other decisions, form patterns of organization, and, perhaps most significantly, create a climate that permits imaginative response and good service on the part of all staff members. While budget constraints, time pressures, and limitations of previous decisions can limit the freedom of administrators in the decisions they make and the trends they establish, their impact is still always strong, especially on developing programs of service.

Formal library instruction within public libraries has existed in some form for decades, but was mainly limited to children in the period when school libraries were just beginning to develop strong programs in this area, or was integrated into other activities and services of the library in such ways as to be almost invisible. Naturalization classes that met at the library often benefited from talks on how to use the library, or library staff members prepared informational materials in response to specific requests. But in its constant effort to be welcoming, accessible to all, and free of the formality of many other educational and social institutions, the public library has usually been low-key about its program of instruction in the use of libraries, and in many libraries, no such program for adults has ever been formally recognized. This is not to say there has not been administrative support to develop such programs, although in some instances that is true. For the most part, however, administrative decisions and other factors have created an environment in public libraries where organization of collections, staffing patterns, and physical aids have, in turn, had their impact on interest in and the need for bibliographic instruction.

CHARACTERISTICS OF THE LIBRARY

While it is desirable to design organizational patterns and physical arrangements for the user, it often happens that an emphasis of one kind entails a limitation of another kind. Such limitations will appear in the organization of the collection, in the concern with human

24

relations, and in reliance on physical helps. Limitations are inevitable and add support to the case for bibliographic instruction.

Organization of Collections

Librarians tend to think that cataloging and classification schemes determine location and finding of materials, but the library user probably suspects that there are many decisions involved in fixing a pattern of finding materials. A decision that encourages one kind of access may limit another. To name a few: libraries that provide any floating collection, whether made up of best-sellers, foreign-language titles, children's classics, or large-print titles, usually provide no clues to their locations except by the designation of space and an approach through browsing; whenever a collection is located out of its usual sequence in terms of classification, it offers special challenges to the would-be user. This may apply to a thriving young adult corner, paperbacks on racks rather than shelves, and precious titles such as car manuals or insurance examinations that are kept in some location of limited access in order to preserve them. Every decision that affects location of materials within a public library affects access and the need to inform the public. When adult and children's collections are maintained separately, the public of all ages needs to be reminded occasionally of resources available in the other location, especially if it must be accessed through a separate catalog. Local history collections, media in such formats as discs or cassettes, and the perennial pamphlets and periodicals are parts of collections to which the library needs to provide some guidance, but it is rare for that guidance to be in the form of user education. Concerning the published guides to collections, such as indexes or other reference materials that require some skill to use, it is widely observable that, often, users do not know about these guides, so they do not ask for them. Since they do not ask for them, the materials are not bought. Since the materials are not bought, they are not used. The circle goes on, but occasionally, when an administrative recommendation or a request leads to the provision of some item in this category, the circle may be broken unless the success of one or two items is viewed as a fluke rather than an indicator of further need.

Staffing

Even in terms of organizing collections, decisions of staff can have considerable impact on use and on the potential for library instruction. Scarcity of staff is frequently cited as a reason for limited work in this area. More compelling than lack of staff is the lack of the kind of staff that might best undertake and carry out a good program of library instruction. There are reasons why this kind of staff is lacking. The emphasis placed on social concerns and communication skills needed by public library staff members has sometimes led to too little emphasis on good bibliographic background, reference skills, and strong background in use of library resources that prepare one to teach others.

Perhaps more significant is the attitude of public library staff members toward formal instruction in the use of the library. This attitude has several bases. Many librarians came to work in public libraries after having taught school or at least after having prepared themselves to teach school. Loss of interest in teaching and choice of another career sometimes cause a gulf between the librarian and any activity that suggests the formal classroom. In striking contrast to school and academic librarians, public librarians see no special rewards or prestige associated with being part of a pattern of formal bibliographic instruction. It has been observed that the achievement of academic status by college and university librarians has been a stimulus for them to engage in instructional programs, and school librarians have traditionally realized that their rapport with classroom teachers as well as their authority roles with children are enhanced when they provide formal instruction. No such positive attitudes toward library instruction color the views of most public librarians and their colleagues.

Even when they resist it, public library staff members acknowledge that there is a prevalent image of the public library as the place for recreational reading, programs designed to entertain as much as to educate or inform, and for freedom for the user to accept what meets a need and to avoid what is of less interest. While it may be argued that even collections of recreational reading are of more value when they are well accessed, there is a tendency to take for granted independent finding or utilization of material in many public libraries.

Reference assistance and reading guidance are valued, and individual communication with users is attempted and often attained even when it may not be economical or efficient. Knowing the community that a library serves usually means knowing and serving that community in a very personal way: saving some new items for individuals who are always asking for them; purchasing titles that reflect the interests of others; requesting from other library sources the materials needed for some specific study or project, to name a few. Making library patrons more independent in their use of libraries often means transferring from the librarian some of the thrill of the search and much of the feeling of accomplishment in finding what is requested. These are perquisites not lightly relinquished, and attitudes of the public, which are closely related to them, help to maintain them.

Signs and Physical Helps

Only in recent years has the term "marketing" been used with any frequency with reference to public library service, but the concepts of making the library's resources visible and accessible, of developing plans for facilities that encourage use, and of highlighting what is of greatest interest or what may need to be called to the attention of library users have been recognized for generations. The art and science of signs have received more attention in recent years also, the purpose of signs being to encourage users to be more knowledgeable and independent in their use of libraries. It should be noted that the use

26

of signs is but one basic segment of a library's program to facilitate use. Signs can direct and guide users to service areas but they are not meant to replace or substitute for basic skills in finding and using information.

Administrative judgment and leadership have had a major impact in the development of physical facilities and sign programs to make library resources more accessible to the public. Because many public libraries are small, their users, even those who come on a regular basis, have a tendency to think that what they see is what is there. Adults who come only in the evening may be astonished to learn of the crafts programs that keep children happily occupied for much of the afternoon on a regular basis, and installation of a microfilm reader or a microcomputer may be unnoticed unless there is some effective publicity for the new service or its location is highly visible.

It should be noted that a continuing shortcoming is that publicity is often poorly planned and inadequately targeted for the public for which it is intended. As far as development of effective programs of user education is concerned, reliance solely on publicity may have a negative effect if public librarians count the results of public relations efforts in the numbers of people responding. In one instance a large public library experienced a poor response to an ill-defined publicity campaign and decided to cancel its fledgling course on library use.

CHARACTERISTICS OF THE LIBRARY'S PUBLIC

To some extent, the characteristics and attitudes of the library's public can be determined from the attitudes of staff which have been mentioned. Many users of public libraries are not self-sufficient and, since much assistance is available to them, they develop a dependence on assistance rather than a desire to be more self-sufficient. Unaware of the full potential of the library as they have experienced it, patrons become unaggressive in seeking ways to explore its potentials as well as their own. The bibliographic tools that make a library more accessible to patrons are sometimes not readily available in a public library, and, when they are, the public may not be skilled in their use or about their own need to know more about them.

Just as the library staff may value their reference and guidance skills to such an extent that they fail to stimulate more independent use, there are library users who prefer to approach the library's resources independently without the aid of a library staff member. Serving the diverse and anonymous public that it does, the public library is constantly challenged to discover who its real users are. It sometimes comes as a surprise for staff members to learn that daily visitors have never held library cards and may not even be eligible to do so. An elementary teacher who regularly visits a public library branch to check out numerous books to use in class may simply be recognized as a frequent visitor who has a number of children at home. Even when easy conversation at the reference or circulation desk is frequent, the communication may be superficial and unrelated to the expectations the user initially had for library service.

Provided they are regular users, both the dependent and the independent patron comprise a potential audience for user instruction. The dependent would like to become independent, and the already independent would welcome bibliographic instruction as an opportunity to increase his or her self-sufficiency. Public library users are not likely to request programs on library use when they are not aware of the feasibility of them or the values they would provide. The library staff, for its part, is not likely to recommend such a program if the public appears to be content with the status quo. Opportunity for changes in these attitudes occurs when a new service or a new facility stimulates the need. In this regard, there is hope for the future.

Introduction of new services and technologies may be the stimulus for offering bibliographic instruction. A new COM (computer-output-microfilm) catalog, for example, may require new approaches on the part of users and, when a tool is new to everyone, there is no reason to be reluctant about admitting the need for assistance. For many reasons, it often happens that the assistance provided is printed information that is certainly a part of the library's formal or informal user instruction, but which seldom provides information for the more sophisticated users who explore the new service on their own, or, unaware of its value to them, underutilize or ignore it.

WHAT ADMINISTRATORS CAN DO

One of the most difficult things for public library administrators to do is to maintain effective, consistent communication with the people critical of and most in need of what the library can provide. It may well be that if the complaints and critical comments of the recent past were compiled and organized, the result would be a persuasive argument for a good program of bibliographic instruction. The short woman who cannot find cookbooks now that they have been moved from the lower shelves, the student who telephones to report that there are no philosophy titles newer than 1965 because he is unaware of the section where books in the Library of Congress classification are housed, the taxpayer who wonders in the newspaper why the library is asking for more money when it has always satisfied her family's needs--these are the constituents for a program of user education. Their names are not likely to be on the roster of a Friends of the Library group, but they may be the true, long-haul friends who provide the climate of change and improvement. The administrator who finds a way to channel their concerns and to respond, not to their immediate complaints only, but to their unstated needs, is fortunate; such an administrator is, alas, also rare.

There is no reason that a program of user instruction must be developed at the top and then laid upon a staff already overwhelmed with work. This is especially true for a program not ringingly requested by the public. The administrator who is at least open to the development of such a program would do well to permit its beginning on a small scale, encouraging the one or two staff members who are eager and interested to give the program a try. The impetus may be the installation of some new equipment, such as an electronic index to periodicals or a COM catalog, or the introduction of some new part of the collection, such as the business community's gift of business reference materials. An orientation program may be the means of discovering what public response is likely to be. Building on that with a series of programs that stimulate interest and use can be encouraged by the administration and implemented by the staff who would monitor progress and reaction and ultimately determine the direction and purpose of a more formal program.

There are apparent contradictions in the options recommended for administrators who wish to encourage user education programs. On the one hand, it is a good idea to let interested staff be the leaders in preparing and conducting such programs, but administrative support and decisions that assist the program will also be required. Providing means for internal review and external communication about the program is in the province of the administrator. Such external communication should result in an appreciative and supportive awareness by others and, more importantly, in the expansion of the program into cooperative ventures. When administrators interact with other library administrators from school and academic libraries or with educational administrators from the schools in the area, they have the opportunity to build such awareness and expansion.

When no staff member appears to take the lead--or, worse yet, when those who are interested leave the library or move into other areas of work--the continuity of the program is the responsibility of the administrator. For this and other reasons the public needs to be made aware of the benefits of instruction in use of the library so that the staff is stimulated by the public as well as by the administration.

Building on success is always the easiest kind of building. There was an era when much library instruction for children was the accepted responsibility of the public library. Recalling that era may give a useful historical perspective to this emphasis when such a program is seen as irrelevant or just "not our job." Integrating user education with a total program of public awareness is an important function of the supportive administrator. Continuing recognition that learning is a lifelong activity may be the most cogent argument for the public library's engaging in programs to teach use of the library. The greatest success may not be measured in the number or even the quality of programs. Integration of this kind of instruction into adult education programs of various kinds could result in acceptance of a slogan that goes beyond the superficial: "Use Your Public Library!" to the more fulfilling: "Know How to Use Your Public Library!"

why can't i find
verbs in the card catalog?
library instruction
in schools

ANNE M. HYLAND

Will you find me a picture of an evergreen tree?
I need an example of a good simile.
Does chromium begin with a C or a K?
My assignment for Tuesday is on TVA.
A diagram, please, of the lungs of a frog.
Why can't I find verbs in the card catalog?[1]

Do these questions from school-age public library users sound familiar? You bet! If you work in a public library lucky enough to be accessible to students you'll hear all of these and more. Some students ask well thought-out clear questions. Other questions need to be clarified. Who is responsible for teaching what to these students? How can realistic instructional links be developed between schools and public libraries?

It is helpful to explore how school libraries came to be, for within that development the role of the modern school library media center was established. A school library media center is not a small public library in a school building. It is only one part of a total educational system defined by national and state expectations, by the local philosophy, and by the local scope of instruction. The school media center must focus its program to meet the concerns the school district has mandated. Supporting teachers' instructional needs, improving student reading ability, and coordinating with other instruction a student's study and communication skills are the heart of why a library exists in a kindergarten through 12th grade educational setting. Once we see why schools do what they do and explore the most effective means to meet these goals, providing links between the school and the public library can more easily be defined.

HISTORICAL CONTEXT

Through most of our history, primary and secondary education dealt in specific information and fixed ideas. The bent of this education was humanistic. Ideas and information could be learned, and would hold true for half a lifetime at least. A textbook could be used over and over by all the brothers and sisters of a family. After World War II science and technology effected a revolution that is continuing. We realized that information was not static after all. With the launching of Sputnik in 1957, American education needed to do a quick about-face. Society sharply increased its demand for graduates who could not only read and write superior prose, but also who could apply mathematical concepts (not just facts) to scientific fields yet unnamed. Textbooks and anthologies were no longer enough. The federal push in the sixties put libraries back into schools and made educational research and accountability public concepts. Teachers were trained and retrained--putting theory into practice--revising practice--revising theory. Perhaps the most notable example of over-hauling the educational system, at least the curriculum, was the introduction of New Math. Curriculum change was to become routine every five to six years in many school districts.

Developing technology and educational research combined quickly to foster the now generally accepted theory that every student was unique, that each learned best in different ways, and that each teacher taught most effectively in different ways. To be effective, instruction should be presented beginning with basic concepts and, with the recognition of discrete learning processes, move to higher levels of evaluation.[2] How we operate intellectually could be described in at least 120 discrete ways.[3] Teachers required more than a single textbook for each student if they were to meet the learning demands, provide remediation where necessary, and facilitate developing learning strengths when appropriate. The extensive use of multimedia instructional materials successfully met the demand. The most pertinent materials had to be searched for, purchased, and made accessible. The need for information remained the same, but the format now became equally important to the educational process. School librarians expanded their basic procedures and applied it to a wide range of information formats.

The library training programs established in the 1900s had been technical programs. Librarians in schools found that they needed to be trained and retrained along with the teachers if their programs were to be responsive to the new focus of education. Students had to be taught how to learn and to continue to learn, how to gather future information that did not yet exist, and how to listen and observe. No one was prepared to provide this instruction to students. The librarians were at least knowledgeable in the content area. By the end of the sixties all state certification agencies expected school librarians to be certificated teachers as well. Each state now has dozens of programs in colleges of education which offer major areas of study in library media, parallel to other teaching majors.

The school library media center is now an integral part of the educational institution. The name change from school library to school library media center, or instructional resource center (IRC), or instructional materials center (IMC), marked the transition from the high school study hall-library room full of books to be used when reports were due, to multilevel spacious facilities where all types of instructional resources are available for continuous individual use by teachers and students. The resources are used in the media centers, in classrooms, as portions of unit instruction, or in a photography lab. Physical housing of materials is not as important as its accessibility. More importantly, trained personnel work with teachers and students on a daily basis.

Local Philosophy

Each school district has adopted a philosophy statement of what they expect their institution to do. This is important and worth frequent examination. In it the elected governing body has defined its hopes and expectations for its schools and students. The educational structure in action should clearly reflect the philosophy statement. The library media program must also conform to the expressed expectations. A media center program in a district which encourages students to "develop to their fullest potential" will use many, many resources in a variety of flexible ways.

Scope of Instruction

The curriculum is defined as "the grouping of learning opportunities planned to achieve educational goals."[4] The "educational goals" conform to the district's philosophy, previously discussed. The "learning opportunities" are the total scope of instruction and the "grouping" refers to the sequence in which information is presented. These three elements remain relatively constant over time. <u>How</u> a teacher presents this information changes rapidly, but the hopes of education, what is to be learned, and what should be learned first do not.

GOALS AND OBJECTIVES

A K-12 education is intended to be a <u>general</u> education, its purpose being to educate adults to live and act with intelligence in the world. Individual students progress through the scope and sequence of instruction in an orderly manner from one end to the other. Testing out of lower levels is possible, but the continuous and step-wise progress toward a predetermined ultimate end is explicit. Students will never come this way again--adults never again will reach for their Open Court Math series, or Houghton-Mifflin social studies text in order to learn a new concept. The K-12 educational program is clearly a process of preparation for later living in adult environments. We have to believe that facts and skills learned can be and will be transferable to other more useful settings in the real world.

Instruction

School library media center programs have two areas of focus: teacher instruction and student learning. The teachers are the institution's employees. In a sense, the school media center is very similar to a corporate business library that must meet the informational needs of its employees. The school media center is expected to supply the instructional resources teachers need in order to carry out the goals of the institution (business). This includes print materials, nonprint materials, and equipment used in actual instruction. These resources must correspond to the expected scope and sequence of instruction, and also to the unique concerns of individual students who learn best one way, who do not learn at all in other ways, who require smaller or larger bites of information presented. Teachers are becoming more and more prescriptive in their task, and the materials they use must match their needs.

Sometimes there are no commercially available resources that will accomplish the task. In those cases the school media center (just like a special library) must coordinate the production of new instructional resources. This can be as easy as laminating a teacher-made math manipulative, or as complex as producing a multimedia program comparing pyramids and Mayan temples.

The school media center also has some obligation to contribute to the professional growth and development of the teachers. All school media centers build and maintain a professional collection of resources. In addition, districts often provide a professional resource center of more expensive educational indexes, handbooks, educational reference items, and journals.

Contributing to teacher professional growth can include actual training sessions in effective use of resources, equipment, or in the various aspects of production. Puppetry techniques, simulation techniques, learning center development, instructional management, or listening and viewing skill techniques could each be legitimate topics for in-service training coordinated by the school media center.

Teachers as specific patrons are part of what make school media centers unique. Media personnel must be able to work well with each member of the staff. Teachers should also be actively involved in the selection of instructional materials. Because a school has a limited population, exact needs can be determined. Teachers are the best indicator of these needs. They are aware of individual learning strengths and weaknesses, reading ability, and scope and sequence of the instructional plan. The more teachers are involved in the selection of materials, the more comfortable they become with using what is available, and with suggesting additional areas of need. Teachers are not trained in the ins and outs of material selection (including textbooks), media personnel are. Teachers know what instructional needs they have, media personnel do not. The two must work together if the media center program is to be at all effective.

33

Learning

Student learning is probably the most obvious area of focus for the school library media center program. The media center is, of course, expected to provide materials for student use. The materials should support the curriculum, enabling students to do research for assigned projects, or explore a topic in greater depth. Resources are also expected to be available to meet the general interests of students that may not be addressed in the curriculum.

The media center program is also expected to <u>actively contribute</u> to the education of students. This is far beyond the relatively passive activity of making appropriate materials accessible. The program is expected to contribute to a student's ability to read, and to develop library study and research ability. Reading skills could be developed. Media center programs more often focus on reading guidance and appreciation. Library skills generally focus on use of "finding" tools and using various parts of general books.

The school library media center must constantly ask, "What difference does it make to the education of students, that I am here?" Focusing on actively contributing to the total education of students is central to the media program's purpose. Educational theory offers schools sound ways to provide a "contributing education."

WHAT DIFFERENCE DOES IT MAKE?

Research has established three factors that affect what and how well students learn. One is that students do learn what they have been taught. This is encouraging. If we take the time to teach the synthesizing of information from several different sources, students will learn. Another more critical factor is student time on task. The more time students spend practicing and exploring information, the better they retain and can apply that information. The other theory maintains that students should be taught in ways that closely parallel how they will apply the information at a later time.

These are three important concepts that should be carefully considered. Students do learn what they have been taught, they need time to practice what they have been taught, and they should be provided ways to practice in close approximations of how skills will be used in the future. Practice needs to be relevant. And it should focus on process. The facts or skills may not be as important as what you did with the skill once learned, or how you found the facts. The way information is presented is just as important as the content to be learned, and is, itself, a content. These theories form the basis for sound instruction in library use.

Five broad areas of instruction were identified after a careful examination of what recognized standards, curriculum guides, and experts expected school youth to learn in school libraries.[5] Figure 1 displays the five basic skill groups and the individual skills within each area. The skill groups reflect the library learning process from the

Organization
   Library citizenship
   Acquaintance with other information agencies in the community
   Organization of the library
   Dewey decimal system
   Dewey arrangement
   Alphabetical order

Selection
   Kinds of media available for use
   Parts of the catalog card
   Use of the card catalog
   Choice of type and level of materials
   Selection from periodical guides
   Selecting appropriate information sources for the task

Utilization
   Use of reference books
   Use of parts of books
   Use of government documents
   Use of equipment
   Using sources other than libraries for information

Comprehension
   Self-direction in reading: literature appreciation
   Reading skills
   Listening and viewing skills; including film/media appreciation
   Study skills: note taking, outlining, follow directions, use of
      bibliographies to locate information
   Research skills: paraphrase information, narrow or broaden a
      topic, selecting a problem, synthesizing information, critical
      judgments in use of information sources

Communication
   Develop bibliographies
   Speaking and writing to communicate
   Production of graphics and other media
   Evaluation of communication products

Fig. 1. Basic Library Instruction Skill Groups

student's perspective. Organization refers to the basic floor plan and workings of the school media center space. Once the student has arrived in a specific location, selection skills are needed to choose the most appropriate resources. Utilization skills are needed to effectively use each type of material. Comprehension skills are those needed to gain meaning from resources. And, finally, any time a student is asked to take information from one source, translate it through personal experience, and give it back to someone else, it is a communication or a production. A production might be retelling a movie seen last week, giving a speech to a class, building a sugar cube fort, writing a paragraph, or taking slides. The student's mind must sift through everything learned, select the necessary details, and communicate a thought to someone else.

These areas of library instruction provide us with several important ways to examine library instructional programs. The activities of the school library media center can be directed toward actively contributing to the education students receive. Some of them can, with a few adjustments, become instructional tools. Displays, book talks, inservice teacher workshops, and instruction in library use may be viewed as serving one or another skill area.

The five areas of library instruction are arranged above from the lowest level skill needed to the highest level. This also, then, is generally the order in which the skills should be presented.

Each of the five areas can function independently of the others. Students can effectively use a reference book without knowing the Dewey decimal system or the parts of the catalog card, for example. It is also possible to construct a bibliography without being able to skim reading material.

The two lowest levels in the skill areas, organization and selection, change (sometimes drastically) from library to library. The third area, utilization, changes only in degrees. Periodical guides have different titles but function the same. The two highest areas, comprehension and communication, change very little from library to library. During the research that identified the five skill areas, it was learned that approximately 48 percent of the emphasis on learning these skills is spent developing the first two areas. The first three areas account for 67 percent. The last two areas, the areas most transferable to other libraries and of most lasting importance to the student, receive only 33 percent of the emphasis. There is a clear need here to move beyond the lower level areas with students and focus the "learning time on task" where it will be of the most lasting educational importance.

This lack of emphasis on the comprehension and communication skills may account for the popularly held view in some academic and public libraries that incoming students possess few skills, if any. Mistakenly (and ironically), their called-for solution to this is usually that the schools step up their instruction in the lower level skills. This recommendation likely stems from a similar emphasis on the lower skill areas when college and public libraries teach users. Without the cohesive quality lent by the comprehension and communication skills, the remedial need will persist.

NONUSE AND NONUSERS

Three or four persistent problems get in the way of meaningful library instruction. The first is students' attitudes toward school in general. They know they will never come back to the K-12 educational setting, certainly never to the school library, and unless content can be seen as relevant to "real life," they often turn off. Second, media personnel often have difficulties providing access to students in ways appropriate for instruction. The influx of a hundred students sent down from study hall is not always conducive to meaningful activities. Third, teacher assignments are often not thoroughly considered. Sometimes it is not possible to answer the question as asked, nor is the asking even clear. If so, then teachers need to be trained, too. A possible fourth factor that can get in the way of meaningful library instruction is the media person. While there are many who are comfortable with all staff and are easily considered as an equal staff member, there are still some librarians who do not venture forth from their centers to recruit teachers or become involved in the total instructional program.

The school library nonuser is also worth considering because he or she, be it student or teacher, will probably also be a nonuser of the public library. While it has yet to be proven, one suspects that the student experience in the media center has a direct influence on future patterns of library use, especially of the public library. Changing this pattern is a major goal of user education. While the student nonuser may not be easily convinced of, or particularly care about, the benefits of library use, the teacher may. The teacher is the key to breaking what otherwise is a cycle of nonuse. My own experiences suggest it is often a matter of showing teachers how the library can be involved in their courses that changes a nonuser into a user.

APPROACHES TO INSTRUCTION

Deliberate systematic instruction assures that students will be taught what we want them to learn. In a media center program this means that thoughtful consideration must be given to how information is presented to students. The casual one-on-one instruction is not sufficient nor can we be certain that all students are reached.

We also have an obligation to educate. While handing a student the material needed to answer the question may be a quick and efficient way to solve the immediate need, we owe students the opportunity to learn that selection ability for themselves. We should also not be so presumptuous as to assume that we always have the answer handy. If this were the case, how would new solutions to old questions ever develop?

It is possible to teach students the skills outlined in figure 1 as a pure subject. This is the way librarians are trained and it can obviously be effective under the right conditions. Library orientation is often taught in this way. In some schools orientation provides the only occasion when media personnel and students meet. In such situations, various means need to be used to make the instruction as relevant as possible. Index cards with questions that can be answered using the card catalog or various reference resources are a way to familiarize students with these sources and provide the means to actually use the materials to answer questions. Even if the questions are very general and do not relate to any other subjects, the exercise does make students more comfortable with the sources later.

Another useful technique is to provide a brief simulation of some sort in order to stimulate student interest in a topic. Simulations involve instruction in the context of a subject. While the topic has no tie with the structured curriculum and may not be immediately useful to any other class, the <u>process</u> techniques will be applicable to other tasks at later dates. In general, it is far better to tie library skill instruction in with content area learning.

Media personnel need to be familiar with what is taught when, in order to make realistic ties. Helping to achieve these ties (and to illustrate the "curricular tie" for the public librarian), a library skills goal is set forth in table 1A-D. This was written as part of a language arts curriculum for a school district. Such systematic preplanning can make library instruction much more meaningful to the student and will invite greater teacher support. The goal (table 1A) shows that skills are logically sequenced and are tailored to the unique concerns of the language arts curriculum. Table 1B-C explains and extends the steps by grade level under objectives II:2 and II:3 in table 1A. Table 1B shows that not all subject headings are discussed, only those which will be useful to that subject area. Table 1C also includes relevant references along with sources of common interest to most other curricula. To illustrate some of the activities leading to the "comprehension" skill discussed above, table 1D describes some general ones for the language arts curriculum. If guides were used in each subject area, it is easy to see that library instruction would take place in all subject areas all year.

In another project teachers developed content-related questions which could be answered from available library resources.[6] The teachers wrote the questions on 4-by-6 cards and provided book titles and pages where the answer could be obtained. Teachers distributed the cards to students through classwork. This accomplished several purposes: students received practice in using library resources, teachers became aware of available library resources and, consequently, became more concerned with the types of questions they asked students to pursue.

Table 1. Library Skills Goal

A. Portion of Language Arts Curriculum Guide

Goal II: To help students learn to gather, interpret, synthesize, and evaluate information.

II:1-Terminal Objective: To help students learn the ways information is organized.
   A. Locate various sections of the library where language arts information is available
   B. Use the Dewey decimal arrangement in libraries to locate language arts materials

II:2-Terminal Objective: To help students develop effective techniques for selecting appropriate information.
   A. Use the card catalog to locate information
   B. Use periodical guides and specialized indexes to select language arts related information
   C. Select information appropriate for the task

II:3-Terminal Objective: To help students learn to use information resources.
   A. Use various parts of books to gather information
   B. Use various types of equipment to gather information from various media formats
   C. Use language arts periodicals
   D. Use information from other sources

II:4-Terminal Objective: To help students develop effective research and study skills.
   A. Use study skills effectively
   B. Use research skills effectively
   C. Make critical judgments in the use of information sources

II:5-Terminal Objective: To help students develop effective production and communication skills.
   A. Develop bibliographies
   B. Communicate ideas to others
   C. Evaluate communication products

B. Selection

II:2-Terminal Objective: To help students develop effective techniques for selecting appropriate information.

	K-2	3-5	6-8	9-12
A. Use the card catalog to locate information			Use subject headings unique to language arts Use card catalog cross-references	Use subject headings unique to language arts Use an author as an author, title, and subject (e.g., Shakespeare)
B. Use periodical guides and specialized indexes to select language arts related information		Use abridged dictionary Use pamphlet files	Use subject headings unique to language arts in Subject Index to Children's Magazines Use specialized dictionaries Use unabridged dictionary	Use subject headings unique to language arts in Abridged Readers' Guide to Periodical Literature Use Master Plots* Use 20th Century Criticism*
C. Select information appropriate for the task		Select a variety of materials for a specific topic	Select correct index for a purpose Select magazines for a specific purpose Distinguish between specialized dictionaries, specialized reference, and general works Select a variety of appropriate materials	Select other information sources to obtain needed information Identify proper sources of information on a specific subject Select a variety of appropriate materials

*See detailed list of language arts reference materials

II:3-Terminal Objective: To help students learn to use information resources.

	K-2	3-5	6-8	9-12
A. Use various parts of books to gather information				
	Use title page	Use table of contents	Use glossary	Use preface
	Use of author	Use of index	Use of copyright date	Use of illustrator list
	Use of page numbers	Use of guide words	Use appendix	Use and understand footnotes
	Use of illustrations	Use of charts	Interpret cross-references	Use appendix
		Locate materials in the index	Use of tables and graphs	Use specialized references to develop and support research
			Use descriptive explanation for specialized books	Use descriptive
			Use specialized foot-notes, appendixes	Use explanations for specialized books
				Use specialized foot-note and appendixes
B. Use various types of equipment to gather information from various media formats				
	Use language master	Use tachistascope	Use equipment as needed for language arts projects	Use equipment as needed for language arts projects
	Use listening station	Use controlled reader		
	Use microfiche reader			
C. Use language arts periodicals				
	Sesame Street magazine	Cricket	Read	English Journal / Media & Methods
(Students should be familiar with language arts reinforcing magazines. Check the individual library for those available and appropriate for student ability.)				
D. Use information from other sources				
	Public and school library	Museums, parks and recreation, YMCA, plays, trips, interviews	Chamber of Commerce, newspaper office, county/court records, state government associations	State library, college library, government documents, professional associations, agencies
	Parents, television, friends, radio, movies			

K-2	3-5	6-8	9-12
Type of information/ format: books, magazines, study prints, AV, opinion, news, stories	Type of information/ format: artifacts, activity schedule, community interests, opinion, experiences	Type of information/ format: business information, community information, genealogy, local news	Type of information/ format: specialized information, detailed information

D. Comprehension

II:4—Terminal Objective: To help students develop effective research and study skills.

K-2	3-5	6-8	9-12

A. Use study skills effectively

K-2	3-5	6-8	9-12
Select main idea	Adjust reading rate	Use definitions	Speed reading
Arrange events in order	Skim to find words	Identify key words and phrases	Underline effectively
Follow directions	Interpret pictures and maps	Identify topic sentences	Use outlines to organize information
	Summarize information from a trip or inter-view	Skim to get overview of material	Use bibliographies to locate information in external sources
	Use guide words	Underline effectively	Infer conclusions from maps, charts, graphics
	Follow directions	Use outlines to organize information	Recognize digressions from main idea of subject
	Use SQ3R*	Adjust reading rate	Skim to find relevant information
	Write a simple outline	Use SQ3R	

B. Use research skills effectively

K-2	3-5	6-8	9-12
Take notes using simple procedures	Narrow (or broaden) a topic		Select relevant infor- mation for a given purpose from within content of material
Answer specific questions simply and without copying	Organize to show sequence		

42

K-2	3-5	6-8	9-12
	Paraphrase information	Paraphrase or summarize information	Limit a topic choice by listing questions or subtopics
		Put together ideas from various sources	Relate specific information to questions or subtopic
		Take notes using a more detailed procedure	Use bibliographies, appendixes, footnotes, and quotations to select useful sources
			Classify notes for future use
			Organize information according to topic needs
			Put together ideas from various sources

*Survey, Question, Read, Review and Recite

IMPLICATIONS FOR PUBLIC LIBRARIES

When teachers do assign topics to students they are of a wide variety and serve different purposes. The topics selected do not always fall into easy categories for researching. Answering "Who else was eating dinner when the Pilgrims did?" is not as simple as it might appear on the surface. There is more to American history than just the materials in the 973s. References to the other people who were no doubt eating at the same time are scattered in library references. But the question is a good one from a social studies class which focuses on the growth of societies. A classification category cannot be a substitute for re-search, yet library classifications must be understood in order to conduct research.

Some assignments lack even rudimentary structure. We can try to make teachers sensitive to this problem, but when you are face to face with a student is not the time to criticize the teacher. "Do a report on _____" is not an untypical assignment. These are generally descriptive reports where information is merely gathered, maybe rearranged and regrouped, and turned in. Every once in awhile school media centers (and public libraries) will find that an entire class must do exactly the same report. Generally 30 books do not even exist on the topic, and certainly if they did exist they would not all be on the shelf. Establishing a quick reserve collection and gathering together all the assorted extra items that might address the topic are quick solutions.

Public libraries must also provide material for school assignments. Their librarians should cast aside protests and cooperate with the school in order to anticipate student needs. The strengthening of collections in public libraries need not be done with school alone in mind, but their materials should be viewed as useful for students.

There are many specialized collections of materials that are useful not only for the adult public but also for many classes. Cookbook collections, technical references for vocational programs, legal mate-rials for business classes, hobby and craft resources, and the like are all available and teachers are sometimes able to encourage their use through proper assignments.

COOPERATIVE LINKS AND ACTIVITIES

A school should develop in a student a realistic expectation of what information agencies can and cannot offer and what the student can and cannot expect to see and perhaps offer at least a preview of things to come. This could be accomplished with slide show tours of the public or college library or television interviews with social services information agencies, newspaper back file rooms, state or specialized libraries, court house recordkeepers, etc. Public libraries could, at the same time, develop their own slide show tours and offer to show them at appropriate schools. If the public library wants to communicate with each citizen in the community, it can use the captive audience which the schools provide to make its introductions to future users. Stress your unique contributions, your special collections, your special programs.

School library programs should help students feel comfortable enough to get past the seemingly insurmountable "library structure" they will encounter when they go to other libraries. A session for seniors might be the best time for this. Point out that libraries use symbols and that symbols will be explained. That reference books have indexes and that subject matter books have indexes can be pointed out to illustrate that there is some underlying order inherent in every library. These are basic facts that we often fail to tell students, so that it comes as a shock to them to find other libraries arranged and put together very differently than the library they have grown accustomed to. The public library needs to augment such instruction by helping students focus their attention on the information uniquely available (or differently arranged) in the public library. Comparisons between the two types of libraries should be continually made in these presentations. Distinction in organizations, subject strengths, and services will provide many topics for the presentation.

Both school and public libraries should continue to promote reading for pleasure as an active and important activity. School and public libraries are the two partners in this reading promotion. Cooperation on themes or activities could go a long way toward an article in the local newspaper, but might make a real difference in the reading ability of the total community. Schools test their students regularly on improvements in reading ability. Wouldn't it be interesting if a public library could do a similar study with its adult population?

A CONCLUDING CHALLENGE

After reading this chapter the public librarian should be familiar with the state of the art in school library instruction, particularly those aspects most relevant to the public library. Also, the reader should now be aware of the library skills schools attempt to endow upon their students for effective use of school and other libraries. And the perceptive reader should have identified several usable ideas for instructing users in the information-seeking and using process. My challenge to the public librarian is this: prepare a list of skills you think a user must have to use the public library, keeping in mind the several skill and knowledge levels, including the ability to evaluate the resources used. Once you have this list, produce a comparable list of ways to operationalize these skills either cooperatively with schools or independently through a user education program. Then, of course, the real challenge will be in acting to improve a person's abilities to use libraries.

NOTES

1. Ruth Street, "It Happened One Friday," in Peabody Library School Summer Directory, 1958. Only portions are used here.

2. B. S. Bloom et al., Taxonomy of Educational Objectives: Handbook I: Cognitive Domain (New York: McKay, 1956).

3. Mary Meeker, The Structure of the Intellect: Its Interpretation and Uses (Columbus, Ohio: Merrill, 1967). This work extended the seminal work of psychologist Dr. J. P. Guilford.

4. J. G. Saylor and William Alexander, Planning Curriculum for Schools (New York: Holt, 1974), p.25.

5. The skill areas are based on original research by the author first reported in dissertation, but later available in "Recent Directions in Educating the Library User: Elementary Schools," in John Lubans, Jr., ed., Progress in Educating the Library User (New York: Bowker, 1978).

6. Jean Leggert, "Library Enrichment Program," Ohio Media Spectrum 32, no.3 (October 1980):23-27.

the
library
and adult
education

using existing resources: the open university experience

SHEILA DALE

The Open University (OU) has often been described as the most important innovation in British education since the Elementary Education Act of 1870. This was the act behind universal compulsory full-time elementary education, although it was not until some years later (1880) that this was actually accomplished. It is a strange coincidence that almost exactly one hundred years later a new means of higher education for all who want it, irrespective of qualifications, should come into being: the Open University was established by Royal Charter in 1969, and 24,000 students began their studies in 1971, its first teaching year.

Before expanding on the Open University, it may be helpful to outline the pattern of education in Britain very briefly. British children begin school at 5 years of age and are educated in various types of schools until aged 11 or 13 years. They may be in the following kind of school:

or
infant (5-7)
junior (8-11) or primary (5-11)

first schools (5-8)
middle schools (9-13)

At age 11 or 13, according to the school system operating in the area where they live, pupils transfer to secondary education, in which they remain until at least 16 years of age. Nowadays 90 percent of secondary education takes place in "comprehensive" schools which cater for children of all abilities, although there are still a few areas where selective education continues. In these areas the more academically able children will go to grammar schools. In 1979-80 over half of all 16-to-18-year-olds participated in some form of postcompulsory education: 16 percent in schools; 33 percent in nonadvanced further education (largely part-time-24 percent); and 3 percent in higher education. "Higher" education begins at 18 to 19 years of age and is provided by a range of institutions--polytechnics, colleges of higher education, teacher training institutions, and universities. Entrance is not automatic. Students must apply and are selected on academic and other criteria by the institution to which they apply. Most receive grants to cover their fees and living expenses. Usually these are assessed on their parents' income. In 1979-80 14 percent of 19- and 20-year-olds were engaged in higher education, mainly full-time. (These figures are taken from the Department of Education and Science <u>Statistical Bulletin</u> London of January 1983.) Therefore, it will be realized that along the line there are many people for whom, for one reason or another, higher education is not possible on leaving school.

A major official education report of recent years, the Robbins report of 1963, recognized the existence of a group of adults who could benefit from a university education but who had "missed" it for various reasons earlier in their lives.[1] In the same year, Harold Wilson, then the leader of the Opposition, had announced his idea for a University of the Air, a university using broadcast media as an integral part of its system, which would enable people to study in their homes. At this time only 6-7 percent of those leaving school went on to full-time higher education, although there was evidence of a demand for alternative higher education in the form of 20,000 United Kingdom students then studying for London University External Degrees (nearly a third of them by correspondence) and half a million other people taking some kind of correspondence course.

The time was ripe for change, and in 1964 an advisory committee was established to consider the idea of a University of the Air. The committee produced a report in 1966, suggesting that this new university should combine the use of radio and television with correspondence texts, practical work and discussion groups, and recommending that a planning committee be set up to examine its proposals in detail.[2] The planning committee under the chairmanship of Sir Peter Venables reported in 1969 and confirmed that the university's main objective should be to offer "a second chance" to those who had been deprived of higher education.[3] By the time the report was published Harold Wilson was Prime Minister, the Vice-Chancellor had been appointed, and shortly afterwards the Secretary. A site for the University's headquarters was established in Milton Keynes, about 45 miles northwest of London and within similar distance of Oxford and Cambridge, major centers of scholarship. Thus the Open University came into being, to provide university level education for all who are capable of it regardless of their age, status or previous academic qualifications. Today some 90,000 adults, most of them also working, are studying with the OU and at the end of 1982 some 57,500 had graduated.

These students are scattered all over the country. They study at home, with some support from tutors and counselors in the University's 13 regions. They receive their course components by mail from the

Open University and through their radios and television screens. For the broadcast media the OU works in conjunction with the BBC (British Broadcasting Corporation). Printed materials form the major part of course materials and consist of "set books," which the students must purchase and read, readers (collections of chapters or articles specially compiled for the course), correspondence texts (or "units" as they are called) and supplementary materials like broadcast notes to accompany radio and television programs and reprints of required readings.

A course unit, to expand on this term, is a specially constructed teaching text, normally including student activities of which many can be self-assessed to provide the student with an immediate check on his progress. A unit normally means about 10 hours of work for the student. A full credit course will have 32 units and a half-credit course will have half the amount. Students usually need to study 12 or 14 hours a week. Courses are prepared by about 400 academic staff based at headquarters in Milton Keynes, together with consultants they may engage, editors from the Publishing Division, educational technologists from the University's Institute of Educational Technology, design staff from the Media Production Unit, BBC staff who work on the broadcasts and broadcast-related materials with academics, and Library staff. These people constitute the "course team." The planning and production period for undergraduate courses is now about three years. At present the University produces some twelve full credit course equivalents each year--the actual number of courses varies from year to year, as it depends on how many are half and how many full credits.

THE OPEN UNIVERSITY LIBRARY

It is within this rather specialized context of distance teaching and publishing that the Open University Library must function. It should be noted straightaway that the Library does not serve students directly, save those few full-time higher degree students who are on campus. Its function is to provide a service to full-time academic staff of the University, in support of the writing of courses and the pursuit of research, and to cooperate with other libraries in promoting the educational well-being of the community generally. As has already been said, Open University students are scattered all over the country studying in their own homes, and the Library offers its services to staff, with the exception of a few full-time postgraduate students. Students therefore rely mainly on the materials provided to them by the University (the correspondence texts and supplementary materials), the set books, and readers that they are required to purchase. For any additional reading, such as that on their recommended reading lists, they must normally use their local public libraries. Some brief notes on this are given to students in their precourse materials, together with a form to hand in to the library they expect to use.

Relations with individual libraries in the 13 regions are conducted by Regional Library Liaison Officers, who are members of the regional staff, usually doing this work as part of their job, along with other things.

HISTORY OF COURSE DEVELOPMENT

The first four foundation level courses presented in 1971 were created as self-contained courses. All reading essential to students was supplied, either by means of set books and readers, which the students were expected to buy, or by means of off-prints of articles provided with the course materials. Help was sought from public libraries on the supply of material for background (i.e., additional but not essential) reading. This involved much public relations work on the part of the University Librarian. Background reading lists were solicited from course teams, checked in the Library, and distributed to public libraries. This function has now been taken over by the Publishing Division, but is still continued as a means of alerting libraries to possible student demand. Unfortunately, it has not proved possible to prepare accurate lists before course presentation begins, so the information always reaches the libraries after the first year's student intake.

In this early period the University was criticized by some for spoon-feeding its students instead of encouraging them to use libraries. Later, courses were developed at higher levels, building on the early foundation courses. Some of these courses entail project work and therefore involve students in independent work, including research in libraries and archives. Moreover, parallel with the undergraduate programs, "postexperience," and then "continuing education," courses have been developed. These comprise, for instance, courses for the in-service education of teachers, courses for social welfare and health service professionals, and short courses of a less academic nature on topics of adult concern, such as "The First Years of Life" and "The Preschool Child."

USER EDUCATION

A combination of circumstances has led a growing number of course teams to include instruction in the use of libraries and literature in their materials: the need to counteract the criticism of spoon-feeding mentioned above; the need to provide help for students on higher level courses containing project work that demands individual research; and the need to give postexperience and continuing education students a means of building independently on to their courses. So far, Open University Library staff, working as course team members, have produced more than forty library and literature guides that have been mailed to students as part of their course materials. Very occasionally consultants have been employed.

The graphic quality of these guides is good; typical coverage varies according to subject and course requirements. The guides contain the following elements:

1. A general outline of the types of library or collection to which access would be useful. Most Open University students have right of access only to public libraries, unless they happen to work in an academic institution or some other organization which has a library. So, they need to be made aware of the existence of university and college libraries, teachers' centers and school of education libraries that offer services to teachers, and record offices and other special-ized types of collections. They may then start finding out which of the types of library indicated are available in their own area. Most British libraries will allow access for reference purposes. It is not usual for libraries other than public libraries to lend materials to people other than members of their institution, except, of course, through the interlibrary loan system.

To illustrate, in one of the guides for an educational studies course, along with reference to strong education collections in certain public libraries, specific mention is made of the large Inner London Education Authority Library, which serves teachers, and of the Library of the National Union of Teachers. To further aid students in the course, a listing of library directories is provided so they can check to see if any local libraries may have relevant materials. Suggestions are made about gaining access to collections that are not available for general use.

2. Guidance in the use of libraries and special collections. This section usually covers some or all of the following: use of the different parts of a book (it should be remembered that many of our students finished their formal education very early); library arrangement--the fact that books have to be arranged in some sort of order, with an indication of the subject headings under which relevant material may be ordered; an explanation of the most common types of catalog; examples of problems which are frequently encountered in using cata-logs--the need to search under synonyms, under broader or narrower terms and related terms, and problems relating to the authorship of documents. For instance, a few pertinent examples of government publications and other works of corporate authorship, and a conference or symposium, are often included. Similarly, if there are known difficulties in the use of particular categories of materials in archives or record offices the author will try to point these out and make helpful suggestions.

Of importance here is that each guide tailors the examples used to the subject covered by the guide, e.g., the discussion of the card catalog or government reports in the Educational Studies guide uses examples drawn from that subject field.

3. Suggestions on how to conduct a search for information. We usually try to offer an outline procedure for students to follow when searching, so that they search systematically, thus saving time and getting better results.

Again, the general, all-purpose viewpoint is focused on specific relevant references to the topic discussed in the guide. For example, the discussion on indexes to periodicals in an education guide includes mention of the British Education Index and Current Index to Journals in Education. The guide for a course on educational administration refers to Educational Administration Abstracts.

4. A list of bibliographical tools or records relevant to the course with notes on their function and examples. Since our students may have to travel considerable distances to a large or specialized library to meet their needs in terms of reference materials, they need to know in advance which bibliographical tools do which jobs for them. On arrival, all they need spend time on is locating the tools. This section is normally the longest, working through the different categories of bibliographical tools, describing their function, and providing an annotated list of samples relevant to the course.

5. Notes on organizations and associations as sources of information advice and publications. A list of relevant organizations and associations, with a note on their aims and activities, pointing up any important relevant publications, is frequently included. This often refers back to the list of journals, for instance, in the bibliographical tools section. There is also an opportunity here to mention any special information and advisory services, and cross-refer with the section on types of library. For example, the guide The Control of Education lists, among several others, the British Educational Administration Society Ltd., its address, and a full statement of its aims including its publications.

The guides are designed to help any student of the subjects they cover, not only OU students. There is now national and international interest in these guides, and some are available for purchase. An additional factor bearing on these guides is that they afford librarians the opportunity to raise with course teams library problems that students might encounter, such as lack of availability of material or awkward opening hours.

As has been said already, there are Library Liaison Officers in the regions, who undertake responsibility for local relations. In some regions these staff have produced detailed guides to local resources: libraries, public and academic, record offices, and archives. Thus, the two kinds of guide complement each other, the one indicating in broad terms the kinds of collection to which students might gain access and listing some particular tools, the other filling in the local examples of specific libraries and other sources. In some areas it has also been possible for staff to arrange seminars with local library or archives staff to explain resources to students. Again, the two kinds of work have complemented each other: the existence of a centrally prepared list of principal tools has saved local staff the need to repeat this and enabled them to concentrate on local specialties.

THE COOPERATIVE ELEMENT

Cooperation between central and regional University staff in user education has already been mentioned, and cooperation with local library staff touched on. It could be argued that the role of the guides outlined above has wider implications. Because they prepare students by indicating to them <u>where</u> they might obtain information and <u>by means of which sources,</u> they decrease pressures on the time of staff in other libraries. This is particularly important in the case of staff in, for instance, academic libraries, whose prime responsibility is, after all, to the members of their own institution, and in public libraries where there may be fewer subject specialists.

Another benefit of the guides is that the staff of the libraries purchasing them are helped in dealing with similar inquiries from students other than our own. The guides produced so far have generally not been so closely linked to a course as to be incomprehensible to people not taking that course. Moreover, the topics studied in courses in institutions throughout the country tend to overlap considerably. Indeed, a number of American public librarians involved in the Adult Independent Learning Project in 1978, when the author visited, were very interested in Open University guides, from the point of view of their use with other students or with self-directed learners (i.e., those wishing to study independently outside the formal education system).

THE PUBLIC LIBRARY IN INDEPENDENT ADULT EDUCATION

Libraries have a vital role to play in continuing education. Some people are able to continue their education only by independent study. They must obtain their books from libraries. That more than this can be done for them has been shown by the Adult Independent Learning Project, which has aroused international interest. This has been fully reported by Mavor, et al.,[4] and also written about in the context of applications to Britain by the author.[5]

Public libraries are part of a network of libraries. Some form of access to all parts of the network is important for self-directed learners, since only in this way are they going to be able to reach the necessary resources. This paper has been concerned with the Open University experience. One might now ask, therefore, has this experience anything to offer? In terms of different levels of cooperation as suggested in the last section, it could be inferred that it has. Some things, such as publication programs, are sometimes more readily attainable by large, or central, organizations with the appropriate resources. If these organizations are producing materials which can be used by others, it is sensible that proper arrangements should be made to make them available. Equally, cooperation in the compilation of materials can be explored.

In the present economic climate it is important that the best use be made of all resources. The Open University's work in the preparation of students to use public and other libraries has been discussed. Could public libraries take a more active role generally in user education? Could they perhaps act as a filter for, or link with, academic and other libraries, where appropriate, on behalf of adult independent learners? In this way, it might be possible for such libraries to be opened up to learners without the pressures on them being too great. Could public libraries send appropriate people to user education sessions in academic libraries? These are some of the questions to be asked on an issue of the utmost importance to adult learners--access to resources--for, in the words of a contemporary critic of the scene:

> The goal of adult learning, as in all learning, must be independence through the achievement of competence and this can only occur, ultimately, when the student assumes responsibility for his or her own learning. The failure of much adult education lies in a general failure to make this fact central to the organisation of provision. Instead we have a perpetuation of dependence on the tutor as the fount of knowledge, partly through the outmoded expectations of adult students themselves and partly through the economic needs of tutors to ensure a continuing class, and hence a continuing income. There is no simple overnight solution; change, in a humane and caring institution, is a gradual process and we have a long way to go before we have achieved anything like the pattern we see as desirable.[6]

Public libraries should be an important element in this pattern.

NOTES

1. Committee on Higher Education, Higher Education: Report of the Committee (London: HMSO, 1963 [Cmnd. 21254]).

2. Department of Education and Science, A University of the Air (London: HMSO, 1966 [Cmnd. 2922]).

3. Open University Planning Committee, The Open University: Report of the Committee to the Secretary of State for Education and Science (London: HMSO, 1969).

4. A. S. Mavor et al., Final Report. Parts I and II: The Role of the Public Library in Adult Independent Learning (New York: College Entrance Examination Board, 1976).

5. S. M. Dale, "The Adult Independent Learning Project: Work with Adult Self-Directed Learners in Public Libraries," Journal of Librarianship 11 (April 1979):83-106; and S. M. Dale, "Another Way Forward for Adult Learners: The Public Library and Independent Study," Studies in Adult Education 12 (April 1980):29-38.

6. J. Wilson, "Possibilities for Adult Education in the 1980's," Adult Education 53 (November 1980):229.

the library learning
climate inventory:
a process for understanding
the adult learner

JOHN C. SHIRK

The worth of an evaluation process is determined by its ability to improve a situation, not just to prove something has merit. The Library Learning Climate Inventory (LLCI) is an evaluation instrument I have constructed to help librarians improve the learning climate in their facilities. It is a modification of Hoyle's Learning Climate Inventory (LCI), an instrument used in public schools to help teachers improve the classroom learning climate.[1] The LLCI is designed to sharpen the librarian's perception of and expand the quality of service to adult learners. For purposes of library instruction, the LLCI when applied to users should reveal the types of learning going on inside and outside the library. Such data could provide a base and direction for a user education program. The inventory consists of a two-part interview schedule, learning sociogram, and respondent's evaluation schedule. The following is my rationale for developing the instrument and a methodology for its implementation.

Shortly after entering the library profession the author was confronted with the phenomenon of adult learning through library programs in adult basic education, English as a second language, and General Education Development (GED) preparation. The extent and intensity of adult learning became more evident through readings of Houle, Penland, Tough, and others.[2] As a result the author devised his own interview instrument and conducted more than two hundred interviews to discover what and how adults were learning. Results confirmed the findings of Houle, Penland, and Tough. Adult learning was discovered not to be uncommon among the selected populations. The instrument was then modified for library use and resulted in the Library Learning Climate Inventory. Why another survey instrument? It provided a profile of the adult learner and relevance of libraries as a learning resource.

Dewey hoped libraries could become relevant to learners. He saw the library as a people's university and the librarian as an educator, concepts some continue to uphold.[3] Where libraries were restructured into learning centers some resisted in favor of traditional services.[4] One observer concluded that part of the debate had its roots in economic, political, and cultural elitism that pervaded society at the time ALA was founded.[5] Traditional librarians were seen to be maintaining library atmospheres that were uninviting to immigrants, mill workers, and the undereducated while zealous innovative librarians reached out to provide learning opportunities for the immigrants, mill workers, and the undereducated. The debate continues.

While the debate continues, studies confirm that at most 50 percent of any given adult population use public libraries at least once a year while from 5-28 percent frequent them at least once a month.[6]

In the meantime replications of Tough's studies have confirmed that at least 75 percent of all adults can be identified as active learners. The trend will probably continue for the middle-aged, and older adult populations will increase even as national birth rates decline (see table 1). More educated than previous generations, those in the middle-aged range (35-50) will be making more mid-career adjustments. More women in the middle-aged range will be entering or reentering the ranks of the employed than in the past, some as displaced homemakers. Older adults will be searching for meaningful postretirement learning activities that can contribute to their physical and emotional well-being. To more effectively serve lifelong learners, librarians could benefit from a better understanding of who these learners are. The Library Learning Climate Inventory can help.

OPERATIONAL DEFINITIONS

For the purpose of understanding the Library Learning Climate Inventory, the following definitions apply:

Adult Learner   Any adult who deliberately attempted to learn something new, who invested time in planning, information seeking, and application of that knowledge, and perceived that the skills attained would contribute to his or her sense of well-being.

Field Research   Survey research that has taken the researcher into the environment of the respondents. Three types of field research are structured (yes, no, or closed-responses only, little feedback between respondent and researcher); semistructured (both open- and closed-ended responses permitted allowing feedback and probing questions between the researcher and respondent); unstructured (the researcher as participant observer unassumingly collects data in a selected environment).

Formal Learning   Learning which the individual took for formal credit including courses required to meet licensing standards.

Table 1. Birth and death rates per 1,000 in the United States

Year	Births	Deaths
1925	25.1	11.7
1930	21.3	11.3
1935	18.7	10.9
1940	19.4	10.8
1945	20.4	10.6
1950	24.1	9.6
1955	25.0	9.3
1960	23.7	9.5
1965	19.4	9.4
1970	18.4	9.5
1975	14.8	8.8
1977	15.4	8.8
1978	15.3	8.8
1979	15.9	8.7
1980 Prel.	16.2	8.9

Source: U.S. Bureau of the Census. Statistical Abstract of the United States: 1981. 102nd ed. Washington, D.C.: Govt. Print. Off., 1981.

Incidental Learning   Learning which "may be acquired more or less accidentally, and without awareness of the learner" until recognized as such later.[7]

Interviewer Bias   An effect that emerges when the interviewer has wittingly or unwittingly led the respondent to answer questions supporting a particular viewpoint.

Learning Climate   The field forces surrounding an individual or institution that have been assets or liabilities to one's learning processes.

Learning Project   Learning which has been acquired in the process of seeking to accomplish a specific goal or purpose.

Learning Sociogram   An adaptation of Moreno's Who Shall Survive sociogram technique.[8] It was used to visually demonstrate an individual's learning projects in conjunction with resources that were employed.

Lifelong Learning   Lifelong learning is a comprehensive concept which includes formal, nonformal and informal learning extended throughout the life span of an individual to attain the fullest possible development in personal, social, and professional life.[9]

Response Effect   The difference between the answer given by the respondent and the true answer.[10]

Unobtrusive Measure   Any low inference or unnoticed method used to collect data.

Valences   Positive or negative forces emitted by an individual in response to one's field forces or environmental needs pressures.[11]

METHODOLOGY

The research instrument in the Library Learning Climate Inventory consisted of two questionnaires, one for the library staff, the other for the community residents. The questionnaires could be self-administered or used in semistructured field research. The self-administered postal or hand-out questionnaire prohibited feedback unless the respondent chose to make additional comments, it could also produce a nonresponse bias, particularly among those whose reading skills limited their participation. The semistructured field research approach provided more robust data in that interviewer probing and respondent feedback were part of the process. The field research approach also had its limitations. It could introduce interviewer bias, respondent response effect, and nonresponse bias. Although more time-consuming, the semistructured field research approach was chosen to use with library staffs and community residents.

To portray the collected data graphically learning sociograms were constructed for each respondent. The purpose of the sociograms was to demonstrate visually to the learners their information-seeking and learning patterns over a one-year span of time. For the library staffs the sociograms were assembled for display to demonstrate how each staff was a microlearning community. Caution had to be taken however to ensure that the presentation of the sociograms was conducted in such a manner that each staff member, learning or not, was not offended. The presentation was designed to enable staffs to build bridges of empathy between themselves as microlearning communities and the macrolearning communities served by their particular libraries.

The author attempted to discover the following from collected data: What new learning projects did the respondent actively pursue in the previous twelve-month period of time? How many hours were committed to each activity? Who assisted in planning and completing each project (self, family, own books, books from friends, books from a library, the media, friends, informal group, paid teacher, clergy, physician, public librarian, employer, business person, and other)? How satisfied was the respondent with the assistance of each planner (evaluated on a Likert scale from 1-5, poor to outstanding)? Why did respondents get involved in each learning project (necessity, curiosity, accidental, influence of another, other)? In what kinds of settings did the learning take place (alone, with another person, informal group, formal group)? Then an attempt was made to discover what the learner hoped to learn in the following twelve months following the same procedures regarding resources he or she would most likely use. Finally a series of questions about library instruction, public library use, and demographic variables such as education and occupation were asked.

RESULTS

The Library Learning Climate Inventory was administered to every member of the staff of a branch of the Houston Public Library, the Bryan Public Library in Bryan, Texas, and 81 randomly selected respondents from the Houston metropolitan area.

Analysis of the data indicated that every member of both library staffs had conducted at least one learning project over a one-year span of time. Eighty of the 81 randomly selected community residents conducted at least one learning project over a one-year span of time.

Eighty-one respondents were involved in a total of 625 learning activities. A case in point was a woman who had been invited by her daughter to become a substitute room mother in public school. The mother recalled her own feelings of rejection in school that led to her dropping out because she felt "everybody was higher and mightier than me." She reluctantly agreed to take the position. Within months she discovered she was being accepted by other parents, teachers, and administrators and that her own children were being positively influenced by her decision to participate in the volunteer effort. It was one of those "incidental" learning efforts that influenced her thinking in the affective domain, a change in attitude she did not set out to make. Many of the interviews produced such discoveries.

Respondents challenged, supported, and willingly assisted the researcher and more frequently than not divulged information not elicited. They also challenged, praised, ignored, were ignorant of, or were openly hostile about public library services. It became apparent through the interviews that the world out there, beyond the confines of libraries, was a world of people who were either driven to learn by events that were within or beyond their ability to control, had been influenced by others to get involved in a new activity, or out of curiosity wanted to learn something new. As a result a profile of adult learners and their perception of public libraries as a resource for supporting lifelong learning began to emerge.

Although data for both staff libraries were analyzed, the author concentrated his efforts on the Bryan Public Library. Information gathered over a one-year span of time revealed the following:

Respondents (from library director to maid): 17

Total number of projects: 114

Average projects per person: 6.7

Total number of resources: 311

Average resources per project: 2.72

Total number of hours: 12,000

Average hours per project: 105.25

Average hours per person: 705.88

Learning activities included hobbies, purchasing a home, self-improvement, auto repair, animal husbandry, pregnancy and childbirth, politics, on-the-job training, religious development, financial management, and home improvement. Activities ranged from 13 to 2 per respondent.

Staff members relied on such information resources as friends, clergy, the library, teachers, counselors, club members, community influentials, and personal books. It was interesting to note how staff members did not always rely on the library as a resource for information even though readily accessible, a phenomenon not uncommon in the information-seeking patterns of adults at large. People seek information from resources they consider relevant to their particular needs.

Christie raised three questions regarding relevance.[12] Relevance to what and when? What could prove relevant at one point in time might not be relevant in another. Second, if a respondent found relevance in a particular situation he or she would most likely remain satisfied with that source: "further items may be disregarded as being somehow 'irrelevant' even though they may in some other sense be more relevant than the ones accepted."[13] Third, relevance depended on the user's, not the institution's or system's point of view.[14] Similar findings were reported in a Seattle study on information seeking.

> When it comes to dealing with an individual as an individual, attributes are but labels imposed by the outside world. The attributes may or may not be relevant to the individual. Attributes are not the reason an individual intersects with an information practitioner at a given point in time. His reasons are situational: the situation is one in which he feels an information practitioner would be useful.[15]

People, including librarians, select those sources of information they think will best apply to their situation which led Dervin and Zweizig to use the term "client-in-situation."[16] Institutions, they said, will become more accountable using the "client-in-situation" approach.

While the inventory provided data from which a profile of adult learners could be developed, the learning sociogram graphically illustrated the learner's information-seeking patterns over a one-year span of time. This was made evident to the staff of the Bryan Public Library. After staff interviews were conducted and data compiled, a learning sociogram was constructed for each participant and collectively presented to the group for their perusal. Comments included: "I didn't realize we had been that involved" while others indicated they had not seen themselves as learners in this manner in that they had confused schooling and learning. Another remarked that she now saw herself as an employee, mother, grandmother, and wife in a learning capacity. A fictitious but representative learning sociogram is presented in figure 1 to show how the process works.

One of the discovered strengths of administering the Library Learning Climate Inventory to a library staff was that the instrument provided the researcher with information about adult learning among librarians and library staffs. It also enabled library staff members to understand themselves better as learners. After interviewing the staffs the author concluded that the Library Learning Climate Inventory would permit each member of the staff to:

1. Inventory his or her learning projects.
2. Become familiar with the instrument.
3. Recognize the staff as a microlearning community.
4. Become more empathetic to those same information-seeking patterns of adults in the macrolearning community.

A limitation of administering the instrument to a library staff was the possibility that communication barriers would be raised between

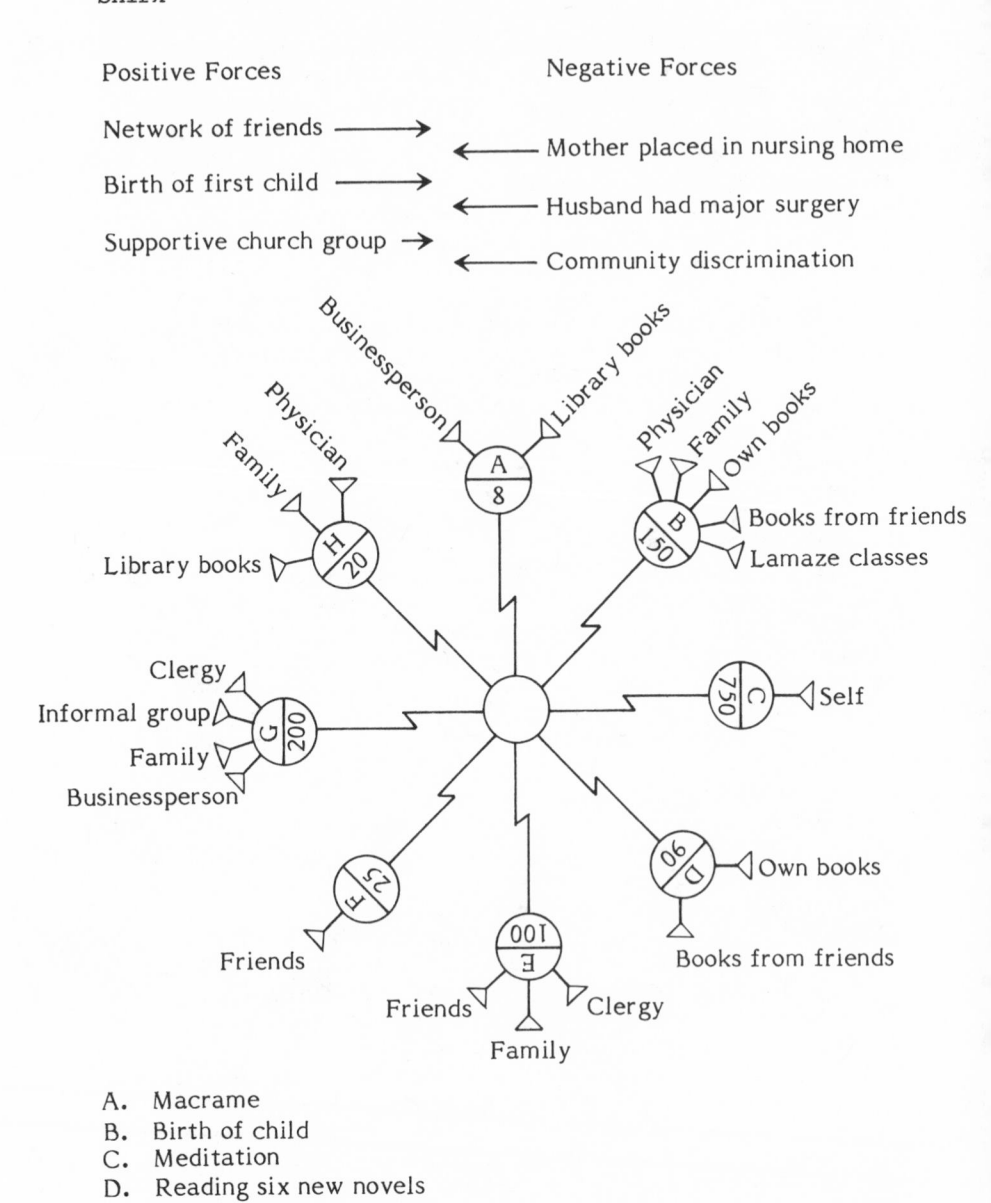

Positive Forces   Negative Forces

Network of friends ⟶   ⟵ Mother placed in nursing home

Birth of first child ⟶   ⟵ Husband had major surgery

Supportive church group →   ⟵ Community discrimination

A. Macrame
B. Birth of child
C. Meditation
D. Reading six new novels
E. Placing mother in nursing home
F. New recipes
G. Improving race relations
H. Surgery of husband

Name of project ⟶ Ⓐ 8
Total hours spent ⟶
Learning resource ⟶ ▽

Fig. 1. Learning Sociogram

professional and clerical staff members, between the more highly educated and the undereducated, and between the frequent learners and infrequent learners. Emphasizing the purpose of the exercise, that is, to help staff members to become familiar with their learning and information-seeking patterns and, after presentation of the data and learning sociograms, how that data represented learning and information-seeking patterns of adults in general, was important. The use of a trained, empathetic interviewer could help overcome this limitation.

Use of the Library Learning Climate Inventory with the general public had its advantages and limitations. Its use in semistructured field research was time-consuming and costly. The advantage of this approach is that it permits the library staff to more completely understand its community. Use of the instrument could lead to the discovery of cottage learning centers and other invisible circles of learning, providing an opportunity for the library to extend its sphere of influence in the community.

Cottage learning centers and other invisible circles of learning could be located in garages, clubs, businesses, home computer centers, churches, community centers, community schools, clinics. These are learning information networks that exist in every community. They are a part of the macrolearning community.

Community teachers and information linkers could also be identified through the use of the inventory. Community teachers could appear as jacks-of-all trades, employers, game experts, block leaders, community volunteers, professional teachers, and business people. Information linkers could include waitresses, community center directors, bartenders, postal workers, gas station attendants, taxi drivers and local politicians. Through these community teachers and information linkers the librarian could also be introduced to a wider segment of the macrolearning community.

Several insights were gained during the field testing and final application of the Library Learning Climate Inventory. First it was discovered that adults frequently tended to confuse learning with schooling: legitimate learning, they thought, took place only in the classroom or other controlled environment. This misconception led them to make judgments about who was or was not learning, a phenomenon that became evident in a situation where cohorts suggested to the researcher that another cohort was not learning based on whatever incorrect views may have been held about that cohort. Second, adults who tended to confuse schooling with learning and had little schooling themselves frequently considered themselves nonlearners, a form of self-fulfilling prophecy. As probes were made during the interviews, significant learning activities (to the respondents) were at times discovered. At this point some respondents introduced a response effect by inflating the number of hours spent on a project. As the interview progressed some would declare, "I'm learning all the time." It was a situation in which the researcher wanted to encourage respondent participation without stifling involvement. The trade-off in information gained versus the response effect was considered an acceptable risk.

Questions that were raised before and during the study included:

1. Why were some persons more involved with learning than others?
2. What influences prevailed in one's environment or life space that caused one to seek various types of resources for their learning activities?
3. Who was to determine whether a learning project had quality, the respondent, his or her cohorts, or the researcher?
4. Were learners likely to use public libraries for certain learning categories more than others (learning categories being vocational, domestic, interpersonal, religious, medical, recreational, cultural, and political)?
5. Were library users more likely to get involved in learning projects than nonusers?
6. Did library instruction appear to have any influence on respondents' use of libraries as resources for their learning activities?

Continued analysis of the data will provide answers to the above questions as well as others that are likely to emerge.

PRACTICAL APPLICATION OF THE
LIBRARY LEARNING CLIMATE INVENTORY

It was earlier suggested and is affirmed that the Library Learning Climate Inventory could be used with both staff and the general public. An alternative approach could also be developed, that is, modifying the inventory and using it to complement the American Library Association's Planning Process for Public Libraries.[17]
Modifying the inventory will allow the librarian and staff to contextually assess the learning climate of his or her community. Use of Planning Process will be helpful in analyzing the library's fiscal, physical, and human resources as they pertain to providing adequate service to the public. It will also be a useful tool for assessing a community's demographic trends. While overlapping between the Library Learning Climate Inventory and Planning Process could occur, an in-depth understanding of the learning community will also emerge. The message contained in Planning Process is to strive to understand the community a public library serves, an aim that is compatible with the inventory. Both should give clues as to how and where library resources could be marketed within the overall scheme of library service.
One could assume that use of Planning Process in conjunction with the Library Learning Climate Inventory should make it possible for the library and staff to become more accountable to the community's diversity: the library staff could develop a methodology for making library resources relevant to the community's needs. Community teachers could be enlisted to serve on library advisory councils; library instruction programs could be developed to acquaint new users with

library resources; and the library could become a clearinghouse for invisible learning enclaves that exist in each community.

SUMMARY

Public libraries have an important role to play in meeting the needs of the adult learner. Adult learning is not an uncommon phenomenon, rather it is a basic drive in human nature. Except in extreme cases every individual has the need to know even if a fear of knowing exists alongside. The need to know is one of the avenues leading to an individual's sense of self-actualization. The need to know is a healthy, therapeutic way of life that can and does occur throughout one's life.

The public library profession has had a vision of being the people's university, assisting in the intellectual, cultural, and social growth of the person. Yet too often librarians found books, not people, their primary responsibility. It is not a matter of either; it is a matter of both. Public librarians have book and in-house responsibilities, they also have people responsibilities. Bringing the two together could make libraries "people's universities."

Working with adult learners can be a challenging opportunity for public librarians. Employing the Library Learning Climate Inventory with staffs and the general public can result in public libraries becoming community-recognized learning centers. Community education, continuing education, independent learning, lifelong learning, and reallocation of education can become realized products of library service. Learning networks can be discovered. Libraries can become increasingly recognized as part of those networks. They can also become increasingly recognized as legitimate resources for learning by adult learners. But it will require hard work, continuous input, and evaluation. Even at the risk of failure, the potential for improving the library's role in facilitating adult learning should make these efforts worthwhile.

NOTES

1. J. Hoyle, Learning Climate Inventory (College Station, Tex.: Climate Research Associates, 1973). (Copies of the adapted version, the Library Learning Climate Inventory, are available from John Shirk, Center for Community Education, College of Education, Texas A&M University, College Station, Tex. 77843.)

2. C. O. Houle, The Inquiring Mind (Madison, Wis.: Univ. of Wisconsin Pr., 1961); P. R. Penland, Learning Patterns of Librarian Clients (Pittsburgh, Pa.: Univ. of Pittsburgh, 1976). (ED 128 016); P. R. Penland, Self-planned Learning in America (Pittsburgh, Pa.: Univ. of Pittsburgh, 1977); A. Tough, The Adults' Learning Projects (Ontario, Canada: Ontario Institute for Studies in Education, 1971).

3. S. K. Vann, ed., Melvil Dewey (Littleton, Colo.: Libraries Unlimited, 1978); M. Dewey, "The Profession," Library Journal 1 (1876):5-6.

4. R. E. Lee, Continuing Education for Adults through the American Public Library (Chicago: American Library Assn., 1966); R. R. DuMont, Reform and Reaction: The Big City Library in American Life (Westport, Conn.: Greenwood, 1977); M. Harris, "Purpose of the American Public Library: A Revisionist Interpretation of History," Library Journal 98 (1973):2509-14.

5. M. Harris, "Purpose of the American Public Library."

6. B. Berelson, The Library's Public (New York: Columbia Univ. Pr., 1949); M. L. Bundy, Metropolitan Public Library Users, A Report of a Survey of Adult Library Use in the Maryland Baltimore-Washington Metropolitan Area (College Park, Md.: Maryland Univ., 1968); B. Dervin and D. L. Zweizig, The Development of Strategies for Dealing with the Information Needs of Urban Residents: Phase I--Citizen's Study (Seattle, Wash.: Univ. of Washington, 1976). (ED 136 791); ———, The Development of Strategies for Dealing with the Information Needs of Urban Residents: Phase II--Information Practitioner Study (Seattle, Wash.: Univ. of Washington, 1977a). (ED 136 791); ———, The Development of Strategies for Dealing with the Information Needs of Urban Residents: Phase III--Applications, Final Report (Seattle, Wash.: Univ. of Washington, 1977b). (ED 148 389); Gallup International, New Jersey State Library, The Use of and Attitudes toward Libraries in New Jersey, vol. 1, Summary and Analysis (Trenton, N. J.: New Jersey State Library, 1976). (ED 124 164); D. L. Zweizig, "Predicting Amount of Library Use: An Empirical Study of the Role of the Public Library in the Life of the Adult Public" (Ann Arbor, Mich.: University Microfilms, 1974).

7. A. Cropley, Lifelong Education . . . A Psychological Analysis (Oxford: Pergamon, 1977), 137.

8. J. Moreno, Who Shall Survive: Foundations of Sociometry, Group Psychotherapy and Sociodrama (New York: Beacon House, 1953).

9. R. W. Skager, Lifelong Education and Evaluation Practice: A Study on the Development of a Framework for Designing Evaluation Systems at the School Stage in the Perspective of Lifelong Education (New York: Pergamon, 1978), 6.

10. W. R. Borg and M. D. Gall, Educational Research (New York: Longman, 1979), 311.

11. J. DeRivera, comp., Field Theory as Human Science (New York: Garden Pr., 1976), 20-29.

12. B. Christie, Face to File Communication: A Psychological Approach to Information Systems (London: Wiley, 1981).

13. Ibid., 51.

14. Ibid.

15. D. L. Zweizig and B. Dervin, "Public Library Use, Users, Uses: Advances in Knowledge of the Characteristics and Needs of the Adult Clientele of American Public Libraries," in Advances in Librarianship, vol. 7, ed. M. J. Voight and M. H. Harris (New York: Academic, 1977), 250.

16. Ibid., 111-271.

17. V. E. Palmour, M. C. Bellassai, and N. V. DeWath, A Planning Process for Public Libraries (Chicago: American Library Assn., 1980).

planning,
implementing,
and
evaluating

JOHN LUBANS, JR.

Successful user education programs usually share some common traits, among them thorough planning and close attention to details. Failed programs also share some characteristics: a lack of or a sporadic approach to planning and haphazard implementation. This article sets out guidelines for such a program based on general planning procedures used to bring about change and innovation in organizations. If followed, they should offer a high probability of success. Lessons learned from my own and others' attempts at user education are also incorporated.

There is a need for systematic introduction of programs--more than a few efforts implemented with the best of intentions have floundered through failure to adequately design or follow a plan. "Burn out," a term that describes the depression that affects the dedicated worker who becomes frustrated, is just as often a result of confused priorities and lack of organizational support as it is of stress from overwork. Jumping in feet first may imply enthusiasm and courage but where one needs administrative and other types of support, keeping a slow but steady course will be more productive. It isn't just the untimely demise of a program that can be avoided through planning; planning can also smooth the way in each developmental phase, particularly for the public library's _first_ program, the one most likely to meet resistance.

Probably the two extremes toward which user education librarians sometimes tend are constructing an entirely original program or borrowing someone else's. It is just as foolhardy to go it alone as it is to blindly adopt a foreign program. To safeguard against either of these two tendencies, two topics have been explored: The first (appendix 1) suggests some of the basic sources to keep one current about user education and the second (appendix 2) discusses the professional support network that exists in user education.

A plan consists of phases that need to be identified in order to anticipate what will be needed and plan the activities to achieve whatever goal we have set up for ourselves. Figure 1 describes a sequence of nine steps for use in planning and implementing user education programs in the public library. Each step is elaborated on in

When	What	Who
1.	Identifying the problem	Manager, Librarians, Users, Other agencies
2.	Forming a task force	Managers, Librarians, Users
3.	Finding out	Task Force, Librarians, Users, Other agencies*
4.	Establishing objectives	Task Force*
5.	Planning the evaluation	Task Force*
6.	Choosing the "solution"	Task Force*
7.	Implementing the program	Task Force, Coordinator, Librarians, Other agencies
8.	Evaluating	Task Force, Users*
9.	Revising and maintaining	Task Force, Coordinator, Librarians, Managers

-steps in planning process-

feedback

*A consultant may be of benefit at this step.

Fig. 1. The Planning Process: User Education

this article. Note that the detail in the steps appears fixed. It will, in fact vary, depending on circumstances and especially on the factor of amenability of administrators and librarians to the concept of user education. Their interest may alleviate the stress on some of the early steps or make them particularly crucial. If people are eager to try out the idea, then there is less pressure on having to gain a group's commitment.

These nine suggested phases create a working structure, a framework which is useful in developing a successful program and keeping it on course.

1. <u>Identifying the problem</u>. This is the reason behind considering a user education program. What factors are there that suggest that a problem may exist? This step is much the same as asking someone, retrospectively, what initially caused them to develop a user education program. Awareness that a problem exists will come from various sources.

> <u>User and marketing studies</u>. (Community analysis) A survey finds a large number of nonusers (or noncustomers) in the library's potential service population. A variety of programmed activities have had no or negligible effect on the proportions of users and nonusers. Nonuse is probably a result of multiple causes; one of these may be a lack of skills in using or awareness of the library.

> <u>User complaints</u>. A frequently heard complaint is that the library <u>never</u> has anything on the topics users want. Reference librarians counter this with the observation that a major reason for this may be misuse of resources.

> <u>Heavy traffic by school-age users</u>. Children typically flood the library, swamp the reference desk, empty the shelves, and take copious notes for their themes. Without denying the explosion of energy, the reference librarian must remain uncertain about the student's skills in information finding and use. Uncertainty is supported by the poor quality of student compositions, their unblushing plagiarism, and dated references often from a single source.

> <u>Redundant questions</u>. The reference librarian notices an increase in the frequency of questions of either a sophisticated or mundane nature. By keeping a record of representative questions it is observed that some research questions are often asked; possibly a teaching effort would be useful in providing an opportunity for users to get in-depth assistance on selected research topics. This same tally of questions shows a high number of biographical questions. It may be that a workshop on biographical sources might reduce the frequency of some of these repetitive questions.

<u>Professional concern</u>. The literature alerts an administrator to developments in user education. The State Library, in response to the White House Conference's call for increasing "public awareness" about libraries, sets aside seed money for grant proposals to heighten awareness.

These situations may represent underlying problems or, in the last case, a mandate to be acted upon directly. However, if it is felt that there is <u>no</u> problem, the resistance to change will be strong. Likewise, if it is believed that no program can effect improvement, there is further reason not to change.

Assuming widespread recognition of the need for user education, it is necessary that an individual in a decision-making capacity be willing to champion the user education cause. This requires an organizational climate that encourages open discussion of new ideas; in this case to define ideas and implement a successful program. In most cases this person will be the library director, except for larger libraries with administrators in charge of the library's functional divisions.

Once the existence of a problem is accepted, the next step is to consider ways to do something about it through user education. Since more than a few people will likely be involved in educating and being educated, it makes sense, both common and political, to gather insights from the people most likely to be participants.

2. <u>Forming the task force</u>. Appointed and charged by the library administration the task force is crucial to the overall user education programs. Members should represent the views of the administration, librarians, and users. The term <u>users</u> includes, besides individuals, outside agencies if they are part of the problem. For example, if the program is to be aimed at school-age users, the advice of the students, teachers, school librarians, principals, or all four will be necessary. Failure to seek representation of those who are necessary to support or to participate in the program has weakened many programs in school and academic libraries. Yet the desire for representation should be tempered with concern about efficiency and manageability. The size of the task force should be limited. One way to do this is for a small committee to interview the representative group.

The committee or task force approach, flawed as it may be, is the best <u>potential</u> tool in countering resistance to change through the involvement of the people who may wield decisive influence. As with any committee, the group may suffer from the ailments endemic to it, such as absenteeism, purposelessness, and chronic discussion. The preventative cure is, of course, a clear charge with deadlines and a strong chairperson who can keep the task force on course and interpret its recommendations, especially those involving decision-making.

The first meeting of the group should be with the appointing individual so that questions can be asked and the charge clarified. In summary form, the task force will find out where the library is on the issue, where it wants to be, and what it will need to do to get there.

73

3. Finding out. Step three is different from the first one of problem identification. This step is meant to examine the alleged problem found in step one and to reveal and to seek out what additional information may be needed. The appointed group now focuses on operationalizing user education; to carry out this relatively nebulous assignment it will likely need to gather specific information to design an effective program. A series of fact-finding efforts may be in order, such as asking users about their library experiences and whether they would be interested in use instruction. Such questions may reveal several potential target groups. Librarians not on the task force may also have insights and suggestions, as may teachers and librarians outside the public library. If, before establishing objectives, the task force decides to do an in-depth analysis of library use and user education, employing a consultant might be a good idea. This person should have a background in user education and sponsoring and conducting surveys, particularly those of the community analysis type.

Ignoring a measurement of what is happening before a proposed solution is carried out makes it difficult to reveal any improvement after. Baseline figures, as they are called, can be gathered to a certain extent through response to a questionnaire or in the commonly maintained service statistics, for example, circulation, reference, and user traffic. If an evaluation will be done, it can be in the form of a "pre-test" of actual skills, attitudes or use patterns which can be then compared to a "post-test." An example would be the frequency of reference questions asked by the target group before and after instruction.

It is difficult without a special research effort to get specific measures of what any one group may be doing or not doing in using libraries. Other measures are too general to be of much value. This can be said about lumped-together data such as total registration, circulation, and reference questions. If available, computer-based circulation systems can provide many variables for study of both book use and the user. Also it may be possible to keep a written record of the types of questions asked by the proposed target group. The amount of time and thought invested in gaining baseline data will depend on the urgency of having such data.

A specific market analysis of instructional needs is another way of finding out what the user expects of the library, what services are wanted, and what users are willing to do to better use a library. This type of questionnaire should list reasonable options the library is considering so that the user is faced with choices instead of having to conjure forth unknowns. Including in the list of selections the category "Other. Please elaborate" allows for the respondents to give their own ideas should they wish to do so. Even here, the listing of the alternatives serves to focus the user's response. Note that the choices listed should be reasonable. Do not list marginal ideas that, while attractive, will not be funded or are not available, e.g., computer-assisted instruction terminals.

74

This "finding out" step basically verifies that a problem exists and defines the shape of the underlying need. In the event that the analysis shows little concern on anyone's part, the project can be stopped or revised without providing a solution for a problem that doesn't exist. Such findings, however, should be considered with the background knowledge that for several reasons, largely the educational system, the user does not know what he or she is missing.

As mentioned earlier the work of the task force might be facilitated through a consultant's expertise, particularly on questionnaire development and surveys. While the consultant should not be viewed as above criticism, there is something to be gained from viewing the consultant as an expert. His or her recommendations become more influential than those made internally.

A trend worth noting in other fields is for the consultant to be more of a facilitator and less of a purveyor of a single solution. As a facilitator the consultant encourages and actively includes the client in the development of a program. In something as complex as user education, this type of client-consultant relationship seems quite appealing.

4. Establishing objectives. This is an important but often overlooked or misapplied step. It can be characterized as: "Once we know where we are (Step 3) we can say where we want to be (Step 4)." The way one says this is through objectives. At best, objectives should be quantifiably measured. For example, if we expect a decrease in a repetitive type of directional question after we've put in a sign system we should be able to see a drop numerically and not have to just guess at it. However, our working towards a goal such as "improving the amount and quality of information found by students for research" is difficult to measure. Objectives within such a goal may help approximate our success or failure in improving the situation. Perhaps we can set up the objective that students will "double the number of periodical indexes looked at in the library." A "pre-test" on how many indexes are known to students compared to a "post-test" after instruction should reveal any differences.

Objectives at the least should be scaleable. If we wish for students to make better use of the library's resources for research papers, we should be able to get some approximation of whether our program has helped by asking teachers about this. The objective here is not as quantifiable as, for example, the factual doubling of periodical index use, but it is still a good indicator of program impact. For purposes of measurement, objectives are comparable to hypotheses. We say that, because of our program, something will happen and contrast it to the "null hypothesis" that no improvements will occur. If we find by use of statistical measures that our objectives have caused change, we can say we've "disproved" the null hypothesis.

5. Planning the evaluation. As indicated earlier, measurable objectives are critical to an evaluation. The objectives will influence the type of evaluation to be done. If we say something "less" or "more" will

happen because of the instructional program, we leave ourselves open to subjective comment. Not only are there different purposes in evaluation, there are various points at which an evaluation can be made. So, besides the questions of how we will measure the program's effect, there, as will be seen below, are the additional ones of why and where.

Why we evaluate, at all, is probably found in the following reasons:

a. to assess the impact of instruction on the group

b. to modify the program

c. to sell library user instruction to others

d. to upgrade methods of instruction

e. to advance education knowledge.

Where (and what) to evaluate is equally vast. We can evaluate:

a. the teaching method

b. the student's performance

c. the impact of instruction on the overall library system or on the public services sector of the library; or,

d. we can even go to society-at-large to see what impact user education may have.

It may be that we only wish to judge the students' abilities immediately after the instruction. However, if we wish to promote user education to others this limited approach will rarely suffice. The ability to decipher a New York Times Index entry says little about how often library materials will be used or how much more important the information in the library has now become. The closer we are to the actual instruction, the easier it is to evaluate. Being able to extrapolate the answer to the larger issues in user education is more difficult. Even without statistical data, asking for opinions can do a lot to help gain insights into the larger issues.

A formative evaluation approach should be utilized. This is one in which, as the program is operating, an evaluation is undertaken and the results are used to modify the methods used in the instruction. At the end of the program a summative evaluation is made.

Evaluation of a single program can be strengthened if there is a control group or a group that doesn't participate in the program but is comparable nevertheless. For example, if a program is done in conjunction with a high school English class there may be a way of restricting the instruction to some but not all of the classes and then contrasting the results for both groups (i.e., the instructed and uninstructed classes).

If anywhere, this step may require a specialist's help. A consultant can help both technically and ethically in evaluating an instructional program.

6. Choosing the "solution." The question now in front of the task force is what technique or method to use in the user education program. As mentioned previously this step is where many programs spontaneously begin, with often predictable poor results. Appendix 3 summarizes the many ways to instruct. One needs to bear in mind these major reasons influencing the choice of the method:

The target group. Is it to be aimed at all users of the library or only adults or young adults or business people of some other distinctive group? How large will the instructional group be? What are the learning objectives for this group--in other words, what skills or understanding will the program try to communicate? What records will need to be kept about the instruction given?

Library resources. Who is available to teach? Will there be funds to cover printing, media equipment, and other costs? Where in the library will the instruction be given, i.e., in a meeting room or in public areas? What media equipment, e.g., a transparency maker, overhead projector, blackboards, is on-hand and available for use in instruction? How convenient are electrical outlets for media presentations? Will the instruction be done outside the library, e.g., in a cable television studio, community center, or in a school? What time of day or evening is the instruction most needed?

7. Implementing the program. As one can see, the actual carrying out of the program is based on considerable planning and deliberation. The emphasis on prior planning far outweighs the actual energy and activity in the presentation.

Since someone needs to be in daily charge of the program a coordinator should be appointed, either full-time or part-time depending on the program's scope. The coordinator's responsibilities and activities would include some or all of the following:

training of library staff for instruction

designing of the instructional package within the guidelines of the task force; creating new programs for use in an expanded program

teaching within the program and monitoring other teaching

contacting other agencies and representing the library in instructional issues (this person would be the contact person for outside groups wanting instruction)

staying current with the user education movement

overseeing instructional equipment and printing needs

maintaining numerical and archival records on program activities.

The coordinator will require time to accomplish this mix of duties. The amount of time largely depends on the size of the program--that it will take time is not in question. If the program is to flourish the coordinator will need time for all of the activities mentioned above. In academic libraries where programs are formalized it is not unusual to see a full-time position termed "library instruction coordinator" at the department head level reporting to the person in charge of the public services division and keeping liaison with the instruction committee.

With the emphasis placed on open discussion of the pros and cons of user education, few of the necessary "stamps of approval" should be withheld. Involving the people most likely to be affected (the librarians and the "students") in planning should effectively defuse any resistance that might have been founded on rumor or uncertainty.

8. Evaluating. It is here that some measure is made of the program's impact. If planning has been thorough, it is a matter of carrying out the surveys, tabulating results, and comparing the baseline figures against the data after the instructional program. Were the objectives reached? If yes, and if there is a difference between the first and the second observation of behavior, then one might ascribe it to the program. However, one needs to remember that other variables can influence the results, be they positive or negative, and that accounting for such variables requires relatively sophisticated study designs. Again the consultant has an important role in creating a sensitive evaluation not only in design but also in interpretation of results. There is a separate discipline involved with evaluation studies with which the consultant should be familiar and able to borrow as needed.

Since evaluation of instructional programs is rare, there is great interest among practitioners as to effects of particular programs. The coordinator, with the consultant, should develop a report of findings that would give substantive indication of the results of the program. Even if there is not elaborate statistical evidence of success one can still gain insights by simply asking people for their opinions and then condensing their views into a summary.

Evaluations should not be viewed as all-or-nothing affairs with the future of the program totally dependent on the outcome. They are useful for seeing how close the effort comes to where everyone would like it to be. And, most importantly, it should give clues as to what changes could be made. Even a program that appears successful will have elements in it that could be strengthened.

9. Revising and maintaining. The task force continues in its guiding role through analysis of the program. Through the evaluation results it can make fairly well-reasoned recommendations on the program. Periodically, it can review the activities, and members can lend support through feedback. Because of their involvement they are the most apt to give an intelligent interpretation to the evaluation results or, lacking on evaluation, readily and aptly defend the instructional program should it prove necessary, as well as give creative suggestions for its development. The task force should report to the library administration the progress of the program and give it its recommen-

dations. Clearly, the more substance and the less subjectivity, the stronger the case will be for continuing, even expanding, the program amidst competing demands and, in some cases, diminishing resources.

Finally, keep in mind that flexibility and the ability to adapt to a variety of situations are critical to a fledgling plan's chances of getting off the ground. The ancient words of Syrius, "It is a bad plan that will admit of no modification" apply to the guidelines in this article as well as any real-life plan the reader may develop.

Appendix 1

WAYS AND MEANS OF GETTING AND KEEPING CURRENT

LOEX   This acronym has been a byword among user education librarians for a decade. Based in Ypsilanti, Michigan, the Library Orientation-Instruction EXchange is the national clearinghouse for library instruction in all types of libraries. Each May scores of new and veteran librarians confer there on a user education topic.

A $45 membership fee brings:

- the quarterly LOEX News, which rounds up the latest ideas and publications in user education. Also it publishes requests by subscribers, conference announcements, and newly received materials available for borrowing from LOEX.

- borrowing privileges for the hundreds of examples of user education productions from all types of libraries.

- help on user education problems. LOEX will search out and provide answers to questions and often produces special bibliographies.

Contact: Carolyn Kirkendall, Director, LOEX Clearinghouse, Eastern Michigan University Library, Ypsilanti, Michigan 48197.

INFUSE   England's counterpart to the LOEX News strives to report international activities in user education. This lengthy bimonthly newsletter, issued since 1977, covers conferences and research and reviews books and materials produced for user instruction.

Contact: Ian Malley, British Library Information Officer for User Education, Library, Loughborough University of Technology, Loughborough, Leicestershire, England.

LIFLINE News Sheet   Representative of the numerous newsletters put out by state and regional committees and clearinghouses, this one is among the best of the genre. Produced for the Library Instruction Forum of the Virginia Library Association, it prints articles, commentary, and surveys along with notes on meetings and the literature for all types of libraries, not just the academic.

Contact: Donald J. Kenney, Editor, Virginia Polytech Institute and State University Library, Blacksburg, Virginia 24061.

Educating the Library User (1974) and Progress in Educating the Library User (1978)   are anthologies of articles presenting both a practical and theoretical view by experts from all types of libraries. The 1974 volume features a wealth of ideas and applications. The 1978 book offers a critical examination of the developing field. Both volumes are edited by John Lubans, Jr. and available from Bowker.

LIRT Another acronym, symbolizes a neutral ground for all types of librarians concerned with user education. The Library Instruction Round Table (more fully discussed with the professional groups in appendix 2) holds annual meetings and publishes the quarterly LIRT Newsletter for its members. It attempts to synthesize current activities in user education and in particular the work of the Round Table.

Contact: Jeniece Guy, American Library Association, 50 E. Huron St., Chicago, Illinois 60611

Appendix 2

THE LIBRARY INSTRUCTION NETWORK

The American Library Association (ALA) has a number of groups concerned exclusively with user education. Attending the meetings (all are open) of the various committees and task forces can be a fine way to meet people in the same field and to exchange ideas with others. Both LOEX and LIRT publish in their newsletters, well ahead of ALA's two annual conferences, a schedule of meetings and programs.

Instruction in the Use of Libraries is a standing committee with overall responsibility to keep ALA informed about user education in all types of libraries. Its appointed members come from all types of libraries and it is the one ALA instruction group that can recommend policy to the Association's Council.

Library Instruction Round Table (LIRT) now numbers over 800 members, each of whom pay a membership fee in addition to their ALA dues. It seeks to provide a "forum for discussion of activities, programs, and problems of instruction" in the use of all types of libraries. Its newness and large number of special task forces and standing committees allow for involvement in LIRT by most actively interested people. Programs are given at each summer conference and usually reflect the Round Table's interest in discussing topics of interest to all types of libraries.

The Bibliographic Instruction Section of the Association of College and Research Libraries (a division of ALA) serves as the forum for academic librarians who are concerned with teaching students how to make the best use of college and university libraries. While the focus is on academic libraries, BIS provides numerous opportunities for the nonacademic to gain insights relevant to anyone teaching library skills. One can choose to belong to this section upon joining ACRL.

Other small and specialized ALA groups, such as ACRL's Community and Junior College Libraries Section Instruction and Use Committee also are at work on user instruction issues.

The state and regional library associations frequently will have user committees, most often as an arm of the college and university section. However, it is not unusual to find an association-wide committee, such as the Library Instruction Forum in the Virginia Library Association. The quickest way to find out what exists in your area would be to contact the state association's executive secretary. Keep in mind that the state media association may be where such an instructional interest group, particularly for school librarians, has found a home.

Appendix 3

METHODS OF TEACHING SKILLS

Workbooks

A form of self-paced instruction, workbooks can be purchased from publishers or developed locally.* They are adaptable for reinforcement use in a class, for example as homework, or on an independent basis with minimal supervision by librarians. The workbook approach is especially prevalent in the academic library for use with large numbers of students (sometimes in the thousands). Much depends on the motivation of the student. A weak interest in the program can be boosted through the use of a mix of answer sheets so that few in a group get the same workbook questions. This spares excessive traffic and (ab)use of one reference tool or the trading of answers among the students. Some academic libraries have perfected the randomization of assignments so that no one gets the same assignment.

The workbook is a visible record of the student's understanding as he or she completes it. There is work involved in reviewing each book--in some instances this responsibility may be shared with teachers outside the library if the instruction is part of a school or library cooperative program. A recent phenomenon in the academic library is the publication of advanced workbooks for use in formal courses, such as economics or history. Depending on the specialization of the target group these could be used in a public library. At the other end of the scale, American Libraries (Jan. 1981) reported the use of a comic book for instruction. These English and Spanish booklets, used by the Free Library of Philadelphia, described a classroom research project to stimulate reading and library use.

---

*These solutions and others with numerous applications are fully discussed in the volumes Educating the Library User and Progress in Educating the Library User, cited in appendix 1.

Lecture presentations

First of all this requires a place to hold the class. Some prefer to conduct it in the reference area in close proximity to the tools discussed. Seating is important and, if not available, most classes will not stand still for too long. Also, this may consternate other users who will either be intimidated or annoyed by the presence of a class. The compromise is usually a meeting room and the books are brought in and passed around as needed; or transparency or photocopied examples are used exclusively.

Time needed for preparation of a classroom presentation can be substantial but it is a necessary investment. At the least, two to three hours preparation for each hour in class will be needed. Double this for the first few classes. This should not be regarded as time wasted; rather the materials and scripts developed and refined will be useful in future classes given.

As indicated, transparencies, slides, films and other media, including the actual tool under discussion can be used in the presentation. While many media items are available, either for sale or borrowing (e.g., from LOEX) many instructors persist in making their own tailored to the needs of the class and the particular library. A compromise is possible, for all but a few items, by adapting for local use high quality materials produced elsewhere.

The lecture method has the one big advantage of allowing interaction by the instructor with several students. However a poorly taught class may totally offset this advantage. The more motivated the group, the more willing they are to overlook the lecturer's faults <u>as long as the content is there</u>. This would apply to specialized or seminar type classes on business tools, or consumerism or the tracing of one's ancestors. The more general the group's interest (e.g., a high school class presentation on research paper strategy), the less charitable students will be to an ineptly presented class.

Cable television appears to offer a wide-open opportunity for presentation of formal (or at least, extensive) courses on information finding and using skills for viewing "at home." Once produced, an effective videotaped presentation can be reused. As a measure of length, some libraries offer introductory courses from 15 to 30 one-hour classes.

Tutorial

Ideally, this one-on-one, teacher-to-student arrangement has the greatest learning potential. The time demands of this method of course make it difficult to carry out in most situations except when scheduled on a specially arranged basis. The user must knowingly and willingly adopt the student role--too often, when using a relevant case study approach, once the student has gained some insights into a particular problem, he or she may view the rest of the tutorial as superfluous.

82

One application of this method could be offered during the time when students are assigned research papers. It would be similar to a term paper clinic (a form of traveler's aid, if you will) given at academic libraries where students make appointments for "counseling" on their papers.

Point of use or point-of-need

This generic term applies to any explanatory device placed at or near a particular library tool (e.g., the card catalog or the Humanities Index) to explain its use. The format can be printed (such as a sign) or multimedia. While production costs and maintenance problems have limited the more sophisticated applications, similar to those found in museums, a wide range of applications do exist. In spite of this, the problems of noise and privacy have yet to be mastered. The ratchety sound of a super eight film loop or one's standing in a crowded public traffic lane with headphones viewing a slide/tape serve to characterize these problems.

The potential is quite great. When properly working and used, this method saves staff time in explaining the use of a particular tool and the person needing but not wishing to ask for help has a way to become self-sufficient. The disadvantages include mechanical breakdowns, graffiti on printed signs, and a usually large initial investment of time and materials.

Tours

These are often mistaken for instruction when instead they are (or should be) limited to help people gain some notion of the physical properties of the building. Mixing orientation with instruction on the tour can lead to a disaster. Such mismatches may be why this form of user education is the least regarded by the librarian. Unfortunately, the user may see, in all sincerity, the tour as a fine way to learn all about the library. When the user wants instruction and expects a tour to suffice, the library should be ready to offer something in its place or in addition to it. Some libraries seek a compromise by giving a quick tour followed by a hands-on exercise in the use of various reference tools. Others have sought to limit staff participation and to guarantee success through self-guided tours, printed tour maps, hanging signs, trails of footsteps printed on the library's floor, and tours on cassette. For the more sedentary and necessarily for large groups, armchair tours are sometimes available using videotape or slides.

Ultimately, tours can be a valuable preliminary to the instructional program and an effective part of the public relations of the library.

Printed guides

Library handbooks and other directional and instructional materials offered to users are regarded by many librarians as similar to tours. Many graphically fine but, regrettably, unread handbooks are available in libraries. The problem relates to the all-inclusiveness of the books that include large doses of public relations.

83

Perhaps because of high printing costs, libraries are now breaking apart the handbooks into separate single-purpose publications, e.g., floor plans, card catalog use, or "finding a book." In this way the user chooses what he or she needs rather than contending with a glossy compendium. Many academic libraries publish single-page analyses of certain important reference tools. These can be passed out in class or picked up as needed by the user.

library
instructional
program
case
studies

virginia beach
public
library

FRANK SMITH AND JUDY PATE

Known for many years as a quiet summer vacation spot along the Atlantic Coast, Virginia Beach, Virginia has had tremendous growth in the past two decades. Not until the merger of the town of Virginia Beach and the surrounding county in 1963 did library service begin in a formal way. With the merger came formal city funding and organization. Since then, the city has mushroomed into a growing suburban community with an economy anchored in agriculture, tourism, light industry, and the military.

The library started several years before the merger as a community project relying on donations. As the city has grown, the library system has evolved as a decentralized branch system with various public and support services located at different branch facilities. One branch houses technical services, another houses extension services and young people's services, while a third houses reference services and services to the blind and physically handicapped. There is also a public law library and municipal reference library at the city's municipal center complex. It is worth noting that the largest of these facilities is a mere 10,000 square feet.

PROGRAM DESCRIPTION

For a long time, Rebecca Mason, the Coordinator of Reference Services, had felt that a library instruction program would be very beneficial. Her experience with the public reinforced these feelings. As a result of her aggressive approach to reference service, many patrons were astounded at the wealth of information available and at the same time frustrated by their inability to retrieve this information. They often expressed a desire to learn more about the library. Not until the fall of 1976 did the Reference Division have the staff necessary to plan such a program. With the hiring of an additional reference librarian, we, the authors, began developing the program. We did not think it was necessary to survey our public to determine if there was any interest in such a program. Our supervisor's intuition proved to be right on the mark! Since the initial program in February 1977, the course has been presented ten times. A total of 226 people participated as of the end of 1982. This number would have been significantly higher if more space had been available. Only once has there been enough space to accommodate all those interested in attending.

The program was established with two goals in mind. First, we wanted our students to learn to use the library more effectively and thereby lessen their frustrations and anxieties. Second, we wanted to use the course as a vehicle to inform the public of the scope and availability of library services and resources.

To achieve these goals we developed a course of instruction consisting of four classes. Participants must be 15 years of age and older. The age limit permits interested high school students to attend, although our program is designed for adults. Since the classes are held during library hours, they are presented only at libraries that have meeting rooms.

The first class begins with a slide presentation which describes the facilities and services of the library system. Since our library is decentralized, we want our students to know that at certain branches they can check out such items as art prints and sculpture, while at others they can get records or talking books and braille. Then a videotape, which describes the steps in our system's book selection, acquisition, and cataloging procedures is shown. The tape enables the nonlibrarian to more fully appreciate the time, cost, and work involved in making books available to them.

A tour of the building is next on the agenda. Special features and services that are unique to the facility are pointed out. For example, when our classes are held at the Reference Division, we describe our local history collection, business information sources, microfilm collection, and other resources that are housed there. A description of library promotional materials, such as brochures and bibliographies that are on display, follows the tour. Each of the participants receives a booklet containing all the outlines, bibliographies, and summaries to be used during the course, including an evaluation sheet which allows the participants to comment about the program.

Following this general introduction to the library, we zero in on the "nuts and bolts" of using the library. The Dewey decimal and Library of Congress classification schemes are discussed first. While our library uses Dewey, the Library of Congress system is included to facilitate the use of the many academic libraries in the area. We want our students to be able to use both systems with ease. The logic and mechanics used in the classification and arrangement of materials are explained by selecting a nonfiction book and analyzing its classification and author number. Transparencies and handouts are used to illustrate the important points.

The second session begins with an introduction to the card catalog. We believe that the main obstacle between the library patron and information is often the catalog. A typical catalog entry is explained with the help of transparencies. Some of the problems in selecting subject headings are described. One really cannot expect a patron to intuitively check the heading European War, 1914-1918, when he or she is seeking information on World War I. Using this and similar examples, we illustrate this problem area and make the point that the library staff should be consulted when difficulties arise.

The major filing rules are introduced in an attempt to explain why things may not be where the patron thinks they should be. Since this is often a confusing subject, a handout is provided so the students can study the rules at their leisure. While we do not expect everyone to understand filing rules, the discussion lets them know that this is an area where they may need some help regardless of how well they know the alphabet.

A discussion of periodical literature concludes the second class. The importance and advantages of using periodicals are discussed and a detailed explanation of an entry from the Readers' Guide to Periodical Literature is provided. The students receive an annotated bibliography describing periodical indexes, including titles of some specialized indexes that are not available in our library but are available in other libraries in the area. In addition, we discuss microforms and demonstrate how to use microfilm and microfiche equipment.

The third and fourth sessions of the course are devoted to reference materials. First, we explain our concept of reference service and outline some of the methods employed in solving information problems. We want the students to understand the extent of our service.

Next, the basic types of reference books are described. These include encyclopedias, dictionaries, almanacs, handbooks, manuals, atlases, gazetteers and biographical directories. We also include books in special areas of interest, such as consumer information, business, career planning, how-to-do-it manuals, and book reviews. Discussion centers around the use and scope of the books. The students are given a bibliography that lists approximately two hundred titles, but all of these are not discussed in class. The list represents the variety of materials that can be found in the library. We certainly do not expect our students to remember all the titles, but we do find that they are amazed at the amount and variety of information and materials available to them. A great deal of flexibility is necessary here as a result of the interest generated by the discovery of all these resources. The discovery stimulates the students and facilitates inquiries into areas of special interests.

We conclude the course with a crossword puzzle (fig. 1) and the completion of an evaluation sheet. The puzzle is designed as an entertaining exercise and is based on the glossary of library terms included in the students' booklets. The evaluation sheet is an open letter to our students seeking their comments on such aspects of the course as the presentation of materials, facilities, and program length.

Fig. 1. Some Cross to Puzzle Over

Puzzling Library Words

Across

1.   Computer-produced list of library holdings appearing on microfilm. (2 words)
3.   Library of Congress.
5.   A printed work of some length bound together in a volume.
6.   Who to know when you need to know.
10. A general periodical.
12. Philosophy of the Virginia Beach Public Library (VBPL) system.
13. Letters indicating which branches or divisions in our library system own a particular work.
14. A _____ catalog is one in which author, title, and subject entries are arranged in separate sections.
15. The COM catalog is a _____ _____ since it records the holdings of all the branches in the VBPL system. (2 words)
18. Has 2 parts: classification number and author number. (2 words)
19. Readers' Guide to Periodical Literature is an _____ to general periodicals.
20. An arrangement among the branches of the VBPL system by which you can obtain a book not owned by your local branch.

Down

2.   A photographic image, too small to be read by the unaided eye, that allows the library to store a lot of information in a small space.
4.   Dewey decimal _____ system.
7.   Material held for a library user at his or her request. (plural)
8.   What you should do when you don't know where something is.
9.   Collection of pamphlets, clippings, etc., gathered together in envelopes and filed alphabetically by subject. (2 words)
11. All copies of a work printed at any time from one setting of type.
12. The listing of a book in the catalog by the subject. (2 words)
16. A publication issued at regular intervals.
17. The place to go when you need to know.

PROGRAM DEVELOPMENT AND PRESENTATION

A total of 200 hours was spent initially to develop the course structure and prepare materials. This time did not include approximately 10 hours necessary for typing, photocopying, and collating the materials. Before the program is presented each time, an additional 10 hours are spent reviewing the materials and method of instruction and making additions, deletions, and changes.

A cost analysis of our program would reveal that nearly all of the expense is in personnel. From a materials cost standpoint, a library instruction program does not have to be expensive to be successful. There is no special budget for our program--we have relied on basic equipment that most libraries have: a photocopy machine, slide projector, videotape player, and overhead projector. Our handouts cost the library $3.50 per person, and we have spent about $25.00 for such items as transparencies, marking pens, and booklets. The cost does not include the slides and videotape that were prepared by the library department for general use. There is no charge for the program.

Publicity for the program includes posting notices on bulletin boards in each library and public service announcements in the newspapers and on the radio. We also advertise by word-of-mouth. In our everyday dealings with patrons we often meet people who express a need to learn more about the library. We maintain a waiting list and sign them up on the spot.

The size of the class is limited and registration is required because of space limitations. Although the content of the program is structured and a great deal of information is provided in a short amount of time, the method of presentation is very informal and relaxed. We encourage discussion and the informal atmosphere puts people at their ease.

In designing the program we wanted to serve as many people as possible. The material was prepared under the assumption that the students knew very little about the library and how it operates. Since anyone 15 years and older is eligible, we get a wide variety of backgrounds and educational experiences. In an attempt to be understood by everyone, the course is kept as basic as possible.

OBSERVATIONS AND ALTERATIONS

When we began to develop our program, a search through the literature revealed little information about library instruction in public libraries. As a result, we started from scratch to develop a program based on what we thought our students would like to know, as well as what we thought they should know. A knowledge of our patrons was essential. A program begun today would be much easier to develop.

One of the initial problems was how to make the presentation of reference books interesting. We felt the methodology used in library school would be inappropriate for our audience, but our experience proved us wrong. By employing the traditional technique of describing individual books, we have had no difficulty in keeping the students interested. We do, however, emphasize the usefulness of the information and are not concerned with the esoteric features that are necessarily discussed in library school.

Although the main purpose of the program is to teach people how to use the library, it is also an excellent public relations tool as well. If the library staff offers good service and indicates its concern about its users, the program provides a way to get this message across. You have the chance to show users how and why the library can be a significant institution in their day-to-day living. Press releases and brochures are means of promotion, but within this program there is dialogue, give and take, and situations that elicit questions, ideas, and complaints. You have the opportunity to listen, respond in a personal way, and convert novices into library advocates.

We have seen through evaluations that these people, even those who are regular library users, really have a very narrow view of the variety of services that we offer. Some did not even realize that they could request information by phone. They leave the class knowing that the library is more than just books and that their tax money is well spent.

We have found that a relaxed, informal atmosphere works for us. We are aware that the library can be very intimidating, so we take extra steps to make everyone feel comfortable. We have a great deal of fun teaching our class, and one of our goals is to make it fun for students as well. Humor and informality help us attain this goal. Flexibility goes hand in hand with informality. Enough time must be allowed for wandering off on tangents, if necessary to answer all questions and address all issues.

Our participants have offered suggestions through their evaluations that have led to important changes in the program. Saturday classes were suggested as being more convenient than the regular evening weekday schedule. As a result we now offer the class on a weeknight and also on two consecutive Saturdays (four hours per class and quite successful). Almost all attended both classes. We had always felt that it was most important to give our class at the Reference Division's headquarters since our most extensive collection was housed there, but our Saturday class was the first to be held in another branch library. We realized that we did not need to have everything in hand to demonstrate. We also reached people that might have been missed otherwise and that we have since seen at our Reference Division.

Throughout the evolution of this program, we have constantly been refining it as best we can. It is always necessary to update bibliographies and slides as new services are added and systems change. We originally started with six hours of instruction; now we have eight. We have tried different evenings, day classes, and most recently Saturday classes. Time should always be allowed for necessary alterations that constantly come up and demand attention.

Another change that has occurred during updating is a shift in the order in which subjects are addressed during the program. In the beginning, we arranged the material in a rather arbitrary way so that it would fit nicely into time segments. This approach is acceptable as long as you can insure that everyone will attend all classes. Experience has taught us that this rarely happens. In response to uneven attendance, we decided to rearrange material to cover the most important things first. Then, the person who attends the fewest classes will still get the most important information. Originally, we discussed using the library catalog and reference books first and saving the magazines for the last session. Although we still explain the catalog first, we follow this with a discussion of periodical literature. We feel that if there is anything users should know, this is it.

LOOKING AHEAD

In the future, we do not anticipate radical change in the basic content of our program, but we do see a lot of adaptation. Qualifying the course for continuing education for school teachers is one possibility being explored. In addition to increasing their knowledge about using the library, the teachers will have a better understanding of what we can do for them. The program could provide an effective vehicle for strengthening the relationship between public schools and public libraries.

Video and cable broadcasting present some unique opportunities for library instruction. A modified version of the program would be appropriate for broadcast on cable television, as well as for playback in the library. Segments of the program could be extracted for point-of-use instruction for such things as the catalog and magazine indexes. With the program in video format, it could be made available to local community groups as a self-contained instructional program. Further on down the line, when most households have video equipment, it could be loaned right along with books, records, and other materials for home use. Perhaps it will be offered to all new library patrons when they register for their library cards.

kitchener
public
library

MARGARET HENDLEY

As a librarian working in the Information Services Department of the Kitchener Public Library (KPL), I noticed an increase in the number of adults asking for information on how to research a topic. I knew that few adults entering a public library intent on research of a subject, whether out of personal interest or to fulfill some academic or business requirement, were aware of the wide variety of materials available to them. Many of the adults we encountered at KPL seemed embarrassed and reluctant to seek help. Although the Information Services Department was conveniently located on the main floor near both back and front entrances, was clearly marked by signs and staffed by experienced, intelligent librarians eager to help the public, it was clear that some patrons would prefer to carry on their research independently, if possible.

This not unique problem regarding our adult patrons accelerated for two reasons. First, Kitchener Public Library is the largest public library not only in the Regional Municipality of Waterloo, but also in the Midwestern Regional Library System. Midwestern coordinates a wide range of services for the public libraries of Huron, Perth, and Wellington counties and the Regional Municipality of Waterloo (total population of approximately 552,000). With a collection of about 400,000 books and over 750 active periodical subscriptions, we serve not only the 136,000 citizens of Kitchener but also meet the research needs of the Regional Municipality of Waterloo (population, 297,000) and occasionally the research needs of those patrons whose own public libraries fall within the Midwestern Regional Library System as well.

Second, the increasing number of adults asking research questions is the result of increased participation of KPL over the past few years in the continuing education programs offered to the local community. Since 1974 courses for either credit or free audit have been offered at the library by two local universities, Wilfrid Laurier University and the University of Waterloo. Much care has been taken by our library administration that the courses offered at KPL will appeal to the general public who are invited to either sit in on whatever lectures they prefer, or register as part-time students and, after fulfilling the

95

course requirements, receive credit. While the library administration does not concern itself with the structure of course content it does review the proposed content to ensure that it is suitable for KPL patrons. For example, courses in mathematics, chemistry, and engineering are not considered of general interest but areas such as history, politics, literature, and business would be appropriate. In addition, any courses offered in the library are also selected on the basis that the KPL resources will help support the lecture content. In other words, university courses held in the library must meet the same criteria of general interest suitability and relationship to the resources available in the library as any other program offered here to the public.

Close collaboration between the Information Services Department, the KPL Community Programs and Public Relations Department, and the representative of the University of Waterloo Faculty of Arts-Special Program Office resulted in our offering certain "back-up" services for these courses. We have maintained a reserve book system specifically for students of these courses, prepared book displays highlighting lectures of potentially high interest, and compiled resource lists of books and audiovisual materials pertinent to a course.

Therefore, based on the demonstrated needs of some of our patrons I suggested that KPL organize and initiate a series of Research Skill Workshops. The introduction of such workshops was readily accepted by our Chief Librarian, Lynn Matthews, as it was yet another step in our already established pattern of offering a variety of programs and resources to any adult in the area interested in some aspect of continuing education. The objectives of the workshops were: (1) to broaden the awareness of the public to the variety of resources available at KPL; (2) to help users achieve independence in the use of various reference tools; and (3) to help users plot a search strategy by determining which reference tool to use when.

Since this was an innovative program, the methods of advertising and promotion would need close attention. It was determined that our target group would be the adult population of Kitchener and the area who were (1) either involved in some form of structured continuing education, or (2) interested in improving research skills for personal or business reasons. The workshops would be open to anyone and, as the questionnaires filled out by the participants later revealed, usually attracted a few secondary school students. It was felt, however, that most of our patrons of high school age did have librarians in their schools to meet their need of formal instruction in research techniques. Therefore the participation of high school students was not actively sought and no advertising was directed at the secondary schools in the area.

It was decided that the advertising would cover three "fronts." First to be considered was internal promotion within the KPL system, including its two branches and four bookmobiles, as well as promotion at other public libraries within the Regional Municipality of Waterloo. This area was the responsibility of KPL's Coordinator of Community Programs and Public Relations. Special bookmarks and one-sheet information flyer-application forms were produced and distributed throughout the system before the programs (fig. 1). Direction, KPL's monthly newsletter, contained an illustrated article about the workshop. A poster was prominently displayed at the main library.

Second, the media were contacted by KPL. Information on the workshops was broadcast over the local radio station as a free public service. A media release prepared by the Coordinator of Community Programs and Public Relations for the local daily newspaper resulted in my being interviewed by a reporter for an article that appeared before the first workshop.

Third, it was agreed that the University of Waterloo's Faculty of Arts-Special Program Office would cooperate with KPL to advertise and promote the upcoming workshop for University of Waterloo (UW) students at local off-campus locations. A notice concerning the workshops was placed in a newsletter circulated to all members of a UW mature women students group. The KPL promotional bookmark was mailed to all part-time students previously registered at the university along with promotional material about upcoming university courses. Lastly, and perhaps most important, contact was made with professors involved in giving credit and free audit lectures at the various public libraries and other off-campus locations in the region. At an initial gathering of these professors, time was taken by the Coordinator of Community Programs and Public Relations to explain the purpose of the workshops and to encourage the professors to promote it to their students. At the initial lecture of each course held in the KPL system, a staff member from either Information Services or Community Programs briefly discussed the upcoming workshop and pointed out the application forms available in the lecture room. KPL's Coordinator of Community Programs and Public Relations saw that the professor from Wilfrid Laurier University, who was offering a course at KPL, was equally well informed and supplied with application forms.

The first workshops held in January 1978 were offered at the main library only with a choice of either an afternoon or an evening session. They were free of charge, but advance registration was necessary, including participant's name, address, and telephone number. (I was happy to have such information on hand when the very first workshop had to be rescheduled because of an unusually severe snowstorm. All applicants were contacted by telephone and informed of the new time.) A total of 66 patrons registered for the first two workshops.

A topical approach was taken for the lecture format of each workshop, which was structured into a two-hour period. Two topics were used as research examples: (1) the subject of urbanization or the study of cities and towns; (2) the author Margaret Atwood. The first topic was chosen because of its possibilities for cross-discipline research as well as its potential for subheadings and cross-headings. The second topic was intended to demonstrate how to find criticism of an author, a research query we frequently encounter. The object of a topical approach was to demonstrate clearly the various possible sources of

97

Banish the Where-to-Start-Looking Blues . . .
Come to a Research Workshop!

Learn How to:
- Find the Latest Information on Anything and Everything!
- Get the Most Out of Newspapers from Across Canada
- Locate Detailed Information from Books and Periodicals
- Assemble a Successful Research Paper or Personal Interest Project

Workshops Are Free but advance registration is required. Simply fill out the form below and drop it in to any Kitchener Public Library location. Registration will also be accepted by telephoning 743-0271, ext. 34 or 35.

Please Check One:
Main Library
85 Queen Street North

( ) Thursday, September 25, 1:00-3:00 P.M.
( ) Monday, September 29, 7:00-9:00 P.M.

Forest Heights Branch
251 Fischer Road

( ) Wednesday, September 24, 7:00-9:00 P.M.

Name_____

Address_____

Telephone_____

Fig. 1. Application Form for Workshop

98

information in the library for the same subject. Time was taken to point out the advantages and disadvantages of each type of reference tool, its purpose, and limitations. The resources used were limited to those available at the Kitchener Public Library although, where appropriate, references were made to those materials likely to be found only in a major public or large academic library.

Each workshop began with an explanation of our divided card catalog and an extremely brief discussion of the Dewey system of classification. The pace and setting of the workshop in a lecture room of the library encouraged questions from the participants who varied greatly in their level of research sophistication. This was followed by a detailed and lengthy discussion of the format and uses of various periodical and newspaper indexes. The Readers' Guide to Periodical Literature and the Canadian Periodical Index were used for demonstration purposes as they are the most frequently used indexes in our library. Other specialized indexes from our reference collection were on display in the room. It was strongly emphasized that the skills learned in correctly using one periodical index are usually transferable to another.

Time was taken to show participants not only how to "read" an entry in a periodical index but also how to fill out KPL request slips to obtain the desired magazine at the periodical counter. Various reference tools for obtaining critical reviews of an author, both current and retrospective, were discussed. The workshop ended with a demonstration of certain special files or resources often overlooked by the public such as the vertical files of newspaper articles maintained by KPL staff, certain government document indexes, and the films and videotapes in Audiovisual Services. Throughout the workshop the import of planning a search strategy was emphasized with suggestions given on where to start the search and what steps to take next. Before they left, participants were asked to fill out a one-page questionnaire concerning the workshop.

Visual aids prepared by either the KPL Art Department or Audiovisual Services were prominent throughout the sessions. Greatly enlarged (10" by 17") catalog cards were shown at the start with heavy use made of the overhead projector throughout the rest of the program. The discussion of each new reference tool was introduced by showing an actual example to the group, followed immediately by a transparency of an actual page from the volume. Then a "blow-up" of a sample entry was shown on the screen. These were created either by using Letraset or by typing with the largest type style available. The transparencies created with Letraset were preferable because they provided a larger and darker print, but as they were costly and time-consuming for the Art Department to prepare in the number needed, typed transparencies were heavily utilized. A total of 20 transparencies was created for the initial workshops. This three-fold approach of showing various reference tools seemed most successful and allowed time for questions from the participants.

A number of handouts were given to all workshop participants. A one-page outline listing the basic categories for the Dewey schedule was given at the start of each session. I prepared two pamphlets, How to Find Periodical Articles and How to Find Book Reviews, which were handsomely produced by the Art Department. These pamphlets contained details of the subjects discussed including examples and explanations of various entries. They enabled those attending to concentrate on listening and asking questions rather than taking copious notes during the workshop sessions. A list of subject headings pertinent to finding films on the topic of cities and towns was compiled by Audiovisual Services (fig. 2). This was handed out near the end of each session as a reminder to patrons of the possibilities of nonbook resources for their research purposes. Finally a one-page questionnaire was distributed (fig. 3). Its purpose was: (1) to determine the most effective means of promotion; (2) to get critical feedback concerning the structure and content of the workshop; (3) to learn what percentage of participants was involved in some form of continuing education and if so with what institution; and, (4) to determine if the objectives of the workshop were met and if these were meaningful to the participants.

The results of the questionnaires showed that we were definitely on the right track, and gave valuable suggestions for improvement in future sessions. One surprising fact revealed was that attendance was almost equally divided between adults involved in some form of structured continuing education and those who were not. This fact, which remained constant in later years, signified that, for many, the public library is truly a "university" where much research for personal or business interests is conducted.

Further innovations came about as a result of attending the eighth annual International Workshop on Instruction in Library Use offered May 16-18, 1979 at the University of Waterloo, Waterloo, Ontario. Although I was a minority of one representing orientation in public libraries, I found many of the seminars offered by my colleagues in university or community college libraries to be most helpful. I soon realized that I had been guilty of the most common sin of novice workshop presenters--overkill. There was a great need for me to simplify what was offered in the workshops. What evolved has been a choice of a Basic Skills Workshop or a specialized workshop.

The basic workshop is still primarily in a lecture format, but streamlined to cover only one topic, that of cities and towns. This simplification enables me to increase the time spent with patrons, both in dealing with their questions and in testing the individual ability to correctly read a periodical entry. Also, a tour of the Information Services Department is included now at the end of every two-hour session, something many participants had requested in their questionnaires. The material on how to locate criticism of an author is greatly condensed and incorporated as part of the whole context. This could be expanded into a specialized workshop if the need is demonstrated at any future date. Also a brief explanation of Info-Search, our com-

Kitchener Public Library Audiovisual Services

Topic: Cities and Towns

The Audiovisual Services Film Catalog

The film catalog indexes the topic "cities and towns" under the following headings:

Cities and Towns
Cities and Towns-History
Cities and Towns-Planning
Cities and Towns, Movement to
  see Rural Urban Migration

City and Town Life
City Planning
  see Cities and Towns-Planning
City Traffic
Town Planning
  see Cities and Towns-Planning
Urban Areas
  see Cities and Towns
Urban Life
  see City and Town Life
Urban Planning
  see Cities and Towns-Planning
Urban Redevelopment
  see Cities and Towns-Planning
Urban Renewal
Urbanization

see also Names of cities, e.g., Toronto, Venice, New York
see also Names of countries, e.g., Vietnam, Russia, Italy

For further information concerning the rental of films on this or any other subject see Audiovisual Services, Level 1 in the Kitchener Public Library.

Fig. 2. Handout Prepared by Audiovisual Services

Research Skills Workshop
Questionnaire

1. Where did you hear about this workshop?

2. Did you find this session - too short? ____
                      - too long? ____
                      - right length of time? ____

3. Did this workshop give you the research information you needed?
    Yes ____ No ____

4. If no, to the above, please explain.

5. Are there any changes or additions you could suggest if this workshop is repeated?

6. Are you enrolled anywhere as a student? Yes ____
                                          No ____

7. If yes, to the above, please state the institution.

8. How do you think this Research Skills Workshop will prove helpful to you?

9. Other comments, criticism or suggestions. (Please use reverse if you wish.)

Fig. 3. Questionnaire Distributed to All Participants

puterized search service, is given to all participants as yet another way of obtaining information at KPL.

After much thought I decided to present the workshop from the point of view of various hypothetical questions and then show how the appropriate reference tools help answer those questions, rather than starting with a reference tool as was previously done. Now, after a brief welcome and introduction, I begin by asking that everyone think of as many synonyms and related terms to the topic of cities and towns as possible. This stress on subject headings right from the beginning, combined with a question-oriented approach, really seems to pay off in the relative ease with which many people, previously unfamiliar with any reference tool, can, by the end of a session, make important distinctions between the reference tools presented to them. This growth in value judgments is an essential step in acquiring the ability to eventually formulate a search strategy to meet individual needs and gain independence in the library setting.

The choice of a specialized workshop was well received by the public. The first offered was one dealing only with the use of periodical indexes. It was offered either as a separate choice or could be taken one week after the Basic Skills Workshop. The specialized workshop stressed active participation among the applicants who were limited to twelve in number. A brief lecture of about 15-20 minutes demonstrating the use of periodical indexes began each session. This was considered to be a necessary overlap with part of the Basic Skills Workshop for those who chose to attend only the one session. The rest of the time was spent pursuing a number of actual subject searches in various periodical indexes. Answers were recorded on two individual worksheets given to all participants at the start of the workshop (figs. 4 and 5). The object of the first worksheet was to teach the use of a periodical index while the second worksheet went on to practically demonstrate the comparison of subject searching in various periodical indexes available at KPL. This latter worksheet was designed so that the participant would start with a general periodical index, The Readers' Guide to Periodical Literature, and end with a highly specialized one, in this case Applied Science and Technology Index. As each worksheet was finished, participants joined in a general question, comparison, and discussion period.

Because of the film appreciation courses presented in the library I decided to try a Film Studies Workshop. I prepared a special handout, How to Find Film Reviews, based on the same format used for the previous how-to-find pamphlets. Stress again was placed on active participation with heavy reliance placed on the New York Times Film Reviews to initiate retrospective searching. A worksheet was also prepared to demonstrate the use of periodical indexes to locate film reviews (fig. 6).

Other changes that have evolved since the first workshop have involved location, marketing, and handouts. In September 1979 a Basic Skills Workshop was offered for the first time at our larger branch library. Although it would be necessary to come to the main library to

Kitchener Public Library
Research Workshop:
How to Use a Periodical Index

Try to find an article on _____ on the attached page
from a periodical index.

1. What heading should you be looking under?

2. What is the title of the article?

3. Who has written the article?

4. In which magazine or journal will the article be found?

5. Which volume of this journal is needed?

6. What is its issue date?

7. On what pages will the article be found?

8. Check the name of the journal in our holdings list. Is this journal available at KPL?

Fig. 4. Worksheet 1 for Participants in Specialized Workshop on Periodicals

Comparison of Subject Searching in Various
Periodical Indexes Available at KPL

Practice Sheet

Subject:

Readers' Guide to Periodical Literature
Subject headings used (include any subheadings)?

Any cross-references?

Were the periodicals cited in the entries available at KPL?

Canadian Periodical Index
Subject headings used (include any subheadings)?

Any cross-references?

Were the periodicals cited in the entries available at KPL?

General Science Index
Subject headings used (include any subheadings)?

Any cross-references?

Were the periodicals cited in the entries available at KPL?

Applied Science and Technology Index
Subject headings used (include any subheadings)?

Any cross-references?

Were the periodicals cited in the entries available at KPL?

Fig. 5. Worksheet 2 for Participants in Specialized Workshop on
Periodicals

How to Find Film Reviews

Practice Sheet
1. What year was this film released?

2. What periodicals cited in the <u>Readers' Guide</u> carry a review of this film?

3. How many of these periodicals are available at KPL?

4. What periodicals cited in <u>Canadian Periodical Index</u> carry a review of this film?

5. How many of these periodicals are available at KPL?

Fig. 6. Worksheet for Participants in Specialized Film Review Workshop

do the actual research, patrons seemed to appreciate the convenience of getting their instruction closer to home. A slide presentation of the layout of Information Services prepared by Audiovisual Services took the place of the tour offered at the end of the other sessions.

Student evaluations made it possible to make some solid decisions concerning the most efficient means of promoting our programs. The poster displayed in the library was the number one "draw" and therefore was duplicated and displayed in our branch libraries as well before each series. Newspaper coverage came a close second. Ads in the local daily paper appeared before each group of workshops offered in September and January. We continued to speak briefly to those taking audit or credit courses at KPL but eliminated any production and mailing of promotional bookmarks.

The effort that went into the compiling and production of the various handouts seemed well worthwhile. The three how-to-find pamphlets are now permanently displayed at our periodical counter and have a steady distribution rate throughout the year. For the last Basic Skills Workshop series I found it more effective to place all handouts within a heavy paper binder and give one binder to each participant at the start of the workshop. This proved to be timesaving and less distracting than continually passing out individual sheets and pamphlets. Each item was numbered and it was a simple matter for me to refer to whatever item was under discussion. Also, a pamphlet outlining the research possibilities at KPL was compiled and inserted into a package prepared by a University of Waterloo professor for students taking courses for credit at various off-campus locations.

Plans for the future include continuing our already established pattern of offering a combination of the basic and specialized workshops twice a year. Plans for other specialized workshops include one on how to research local history using KPL resources, how to pursue a genealogical search, and how to locate criticism of a given film using clips from our own film collection. There has also been discussion on the possibility of videotaping the lecture format of the Basic Skills Workshop using staff from KPL's Audiovisual Services, working cooperatively with staff and equipment from the Midwestern Regional Library.

I feel that our research workshops offer a valuable service to the public. The attendance of approximately 60 people every time such a series is offered indicates that our patrons agree. We were correct in surmising that many adults would like to know how to properly utilize the various resources available in our library and that they would take advantage of a program aimed at helping them gain independence in doing research.

This program has proven successful for three reasons. First, the workshops were created in response to a need articulated by an increasing number of adults using the library. We gambled that this was the tip of the iceberg and that if a Research Skills Workshop was presented it would attract a good number of participants. This has proven to be true.

Second, and obviously linked to the above, is the commitment of KPL to participation in the continuing education options offered in this community. Adults are accustomed to coming to this library to attend a variety of lectures offered for audit or credit from September through June. It is natural for them to look to us for help in utilizing library resources in relation to the subjects discussed at these lectures.

Also, KPL has been involved in the creation and continuance of W.R.A.C.E. (Waterloo Region Association for Continuing Education) since 1980. This organization, which includes participants from two local universities, a community college, the Y.W.C.A., the Y.M.C.A., Board of Education, and the local Parks and Recreation Department as well as KPL, meets monthly to develop and maintain improved channels of communication among the providers and users of continuing education. It also encourages cooperative ventures among members and concerns itself with the promotion of continuing education in the region. The Coordinator of Community Programs and Public Relations and I have represented KPL at these meetings.

Third is the role the library plays in the community as a whole. This is a most difficult matter to gauge accurately. However, a city survey of citizens in 1980 revealed that public library service ranked the highest in quality of 19 municipal services listed. This, coupled with the fact that Kitchener has long held the reputation of having one of the highest per capita circulations in Canada, puts us in a positive and high profile position.

I do think it essential that any such program be offered in the total context of the library's commitment to helping patrons meet their research needs. This implies that the library itself be one whose resources are rich enough that it is already utilized as a research center. Each library would have to judge this individually in relation to its holdings, usage, and proximity to and relationship and interaction with other libraries of all types in the area. It is also essential that such a program receive the full backing of the library administration. Certainly without the expertise and full support of the Community Programs and Public Relations Department, Audiovisual Services and the Art Department at KPL I would never have been able to present the workshops in the manner previously described.

ramsey
public
library

ANN SCARPELLINO

In general terms, the sphere of library use can be divided into reading for pleasure and reading for information. While the dividing line is not clear and there is considerable overlap between the two hemispheres, public service programs often emphasize one or the other type of reading.

As such the decision to stress one over the other can lead to professional conflict. Are librarians to emphasize teaching a love of reading or teaching the skills to find and use the information in the library? Margaret Edwards, the dean of young adult librarians, has championed reading for the sake of reading and has questioned the value of user education. She says:

> With Zindel's Pigman, Remarque's All Quiet on the Western Front, Wright's Black Boy, and Tolstoy's Anna Karenina crying out for an introduction to eager youth, what a waste to anesthetize kids, who possibly are already numbed by their experience in the school library, with a deadening shot of the Novocaine of the catalog.[1]

At the Ramsey (New Jersey) Public Library we've opted not to choose one area over the other. Rather, we believe that reading and research complement and facilitate each other. This conclusion is based on a conviction that feeling at home in the library, even proprietary about it, leads to increased use of the library for both reading and research. We aim to make people feel at home here. And school-library cooperative programs, we think, have indirectly led to our steady rise in circulation, in the face of a diminishing school population.

It should be added that our community is library-oriented. A modern library was the first new public building to be built, other than schools, in the last four decades, antedating a new police station, and in spite of the fact that municipal offices are still housed in an old school building.

READING

The approach used to develop a love of reading, in as many young people as possible, could be termed shotgun. The approach is very diversified and is based on the belief that children who love to read have been read to when young. For example, this year an elaborate display aimed at parents showed our stuffed animals being "read to" by an oversize Babar. It was accompanied by a list of 10 Reasons to Read to Your Child.

One of our programs is a preschool story hour with coffee for the parents, who are encouraged to take the time to select books to read to their children and add them to the books the children themselves select as part of the story hour program.

We have also had a program, attended by parents, the learning coordinator for the public school whose specialty is teaching reading, and school librarians, to discuss what makes children love to read.

And we have a leaflet listing 33 books for children under 12 with the offer:

> If you are twelve or under, a Ramsey Public Library card-holder, and have read them all, see Mrs. Scarpellino, tell her a little bit about each one, and pick up your Library Reading Patch, to be sewn on to your jacket, shirt, or what have you. Free, of course, as long as they last!

Our summer reading and hobby clubs bring droves of young people into the library when school is out.

Since most children under the third grade level live far away and are too young to walk or ride a bike to the library, our approach involves getting the parents to bring them in. Each year an article in the paper encourages parents to spend a quiet hour in the library with their children each week. After the article appears, we are inundated with parents and children. We think we are succeeding with them in developing the library habit.

RESEARCH

How to get them into the library when they are older? Cooperation with the schools is the best way. Particularly when the students have course work requiring library research. Class visits by all third and fifth grades in the community enable us to reach nearly every child at some point.

Eight years ago in Ramsey the only cooperative programs we had with the schools were third grade visits, where the classes were simply shown a film and taken on a brief library tour. In my first year we initiated a library treasure hunt to replace the film. It went over well with both children and teachers who assisted. A year later, the learning coordinator for Ramsey schools suggested that a visit at another grade level, in addition to the third grade visit, would be appreciated. We developed a pilot program for fifth graders which was carried out with three classes the first year, and subsequently spread to all eleven classes the following year. Since each class has about 25 young people in it, the total number in the third and fifth grades reached by these programs alone is 550. In some cases, the school librarians have come along to assist with a class. Apart from this, contact with school librarians occurs at least once a year when we visit them and ask them to hand out leaflets to all new students, telling them that they are entitled to a free library card at Ramsey Public Library, and asking them to stop in with a parent or guardian to pick it up. In the last two years, we also have enlisted school librarians to pass out invitations to their dedicated readers to join the February March of Dimes Reading Olympics. In addition, the schools encourage us to come over each spring and talk about our summer reading club, which has about a hundred participants each year. Contact with the schools seems to grow exponentially and has led to invitations to do booktalks and storytelling during various day-long community-involved programs at the schools.

In our effort to introduce young people to the use of the library and joys of research, we have developed the following three games, used variously for third, fifth, and eighth grade class visits.

Our Third Grade Treasure Hunt takes about 45 minutes (appendix 1). Words are written on small pieces of paper and planted around the library. A list of clues guides the hunter to them. The student then makes a sentence from them. The sentence can be different each year. The first one we came up with was: Being Smart Is Knowing How to Look for Answers. The badge that all students win is made of a gold notary seal (found in office supply stores) with two snippets of ribbon taped to the back, hanging down below. For maximum success, and to make sure each child finishes, there should be at least four people (teachers and librarians) helping each class of 25. The game is preceded by a tour of the children's library. The class is then divided into four groups so that they do not all start at the same point. With help they can <u>all</u> finish. If for some reason any do not, we let them know that they can come in any day after school and finish, so that the search is fun, not frantic or frustrating.

The Fifth Grade Mission Impossible game (appendix 2) takes about 90 minutes, and also requires four teachers or librarians to help. (The classes often come with room mothers who can substitute.) The game is not generally finished by the whole class, hence the name. One or two children in a class may finish with a perfect score. We have small prizes for them, and bookmarks for everyone. We use special stickers (or gold stars) to signify that the answers are all correct when they have gone back and corrected their mistakes, as most do, when they have time.

The tour that precedes this game covers the adult reference section, which students are beginning to use in the fifth grade. Many of the last nine questions can be answered orally by a librarian. In this way, we teach them to approach a librarian (which is really the name of the game). We spend a great deal of time explaining the <u>Readers' Guide to Periodical Literature</u>, since that is the most difficult reference book they will use in the search. We also put each reference book to be used on a different table where it must remain while the game is going on, to avoid having books disappear behind bookcases or being reshelved in the wrong spot. The group is split so that they do not all start in the same place, though they will be working in groups to some extent. When working in a group, they take turns looking up the answers, so that each has at least one chance to use the reference book. The particular reference books used were chosen because most adults need to consult them at some point, and the material in them is entertaining.

In both games, we all but tell them the answers, as they search them out, the point being not to stump them, but to help them succeed and enjoy themselves.

By the time they have completed the fifth grade visit, children know their way around the public library, are not afraid to ask for help, and find research exciting.

This game has been used successfully by the school in the ninth grade. Caution: it needs to be rewritten every few years.

The Library Research Game (appendix 3) has been used by us with some eighth grade classes--usually the brighter groups. Actually, it could be used with any high school or college-level classes where basic research skills are being taught. The encyclopedia is emphasized here because we value it as a first step in research, even though we know some teachers resist its use.

The game should be handed out to all students in a form modified by each library to correspond to its own arrangement of sources. It requires anywhere from two to three hours, and at least three adults to circulate among the young people, helping them as much as possible. Before the game starts, the teacher can, as has been done here, introduce the research paper. After the game steps are completed, research can be completed at some future time, and the paper written and handed in. The reward of this game is in the successful completion of the research. It is essential that topics be chosen before the start of the game, and it is helpful if the topics are the sort that can be found in the encyclopedia. Ideally, librarians would help in choosing topics, doing a cursory research job to be sure that the research will bear fruit. Again, we believe in programming success into a game like this.

In cooperating with the schools, we have encountered some problems and partial answers to them, which may have universal application. Why don't teachers encourage use of the encyclopedias? Because a large number of young people, the ones who don't actually plagiarize the articles entirely, would probably go no further for their information. On the other hand, there is no easy way to combat plagiarism (a knowledge of the student's ability level and writing style may be your only clue) and books, too, may be plagiarized.

Too many young people come into the library needing to find out, but knowing nothing about say, Henry VIII, the Sumerians, or the mastodon.

The encyclopedia is a tool that can be used initially by a student, working alone, to place the topic in time, country of origin, or within broad-based subjects which he can then use to search the card catalog for books on his topic. The encyclopedia, in short, is the preferred tool for the young person with no background of knowledge in the subject to find more detailed works as needed. But the young, who are most likely to lack that knowledge, are the very ones who are not allowed to use it. Whenever the opportunity comes up we try to disabuse individual teachers of their ill esteem. We point out that the information in the encyclopedia is but a point of departure. The data in it are to be used in some new way in any sound assignment. We find that most teachers, particularly those involved in our library instruction program, express a new appreciation for the use of the encyclopedia by students.

In other situations, we find ourselves doing an end run around the "opposition." When a student comes in with, say, a Henry VIII assignment, and insists that the teacher will not allow the use of the encyclopedia, one way to handle the problem is to smile and firmly state that "I (the librarian) need to consult the encyclopedia to find out such facts as when and where Henry VIII lived, what are the larger topics under which books about him may be listed in the card catalog, and whether there are famous people with whom he is associated whose biographies might yield information that will contribute to ideas."

A desirable strategy is to appear at the teacher's meeting early in the year in order to suggest areas of cooperation. We explain the proper place of the encyclopedia when our assistant director speaks to new teachers in our school system at the beginning of the year. We address the question of advance notice about class assignments. Why don't the teachers let us know in advance when they are making assignments to a whole class that involve a limited number of books? The amount of preparation many teachers go through to plan, assign, and assess work is monumental. Having to get in touch with the librarian is something most of them just don't have the time to do. We distribute mimeographed, addressed cards that teachers can fill out and send in with a student or drop in a mailbox, indicating the assignment, date due, and number of students participating. This may, and often does, make life easier for the classroom teacher. We distribute them to the school librarians, who hand them out. When the public librarian receives the card, the appropriate books are put on overnight or one-week reserve on a special table, indicated by the sign: School Assignments.

Why don't people ask us what it is they want to know? One of the main problems in both adult and children's research is the reader who asks us if we have a certain book--the one he thinks the information will be in--and, if we say we do not, sadly leaves, his question unanswered. Or, worse, looks it up in the card catalog, and leaves when it is not listed under the heading that occurs to him. There are innumerable ways of finding answers, and anyone, including the librarian, needs suggestions from time to time as to new ways of looking. Additionally, of course, one well-kept library secret is that the morass of subject headings in the catalog is a problem that discomfits experienced reference librarians (Sears notwithstanding) almost as much as it does the patron. We also never take a patron's word that something "is not in the card catalog." More than 50 percent of the time, another look proves that it is. One suggests delicately that this card catalog is very difficult to use, and looks it up again. Most of the public are only slightly less afraid of the card catalog than they are of the librarian. The sign Please Bother Me, borrowed from the Altoona, Pennsylvania library, placed prominently on the librarian's desk, removes a lot of patron inhibitions.

Why can't young people find anything in the card catalog? Teachers in the elementary grades reteach alphabetizing each year for several years, with mixed results. If the truth be known, a lot of adults, including some beginning librarians, are still singing the alphabet song around the J's and K's in the card catalog. The card catalog has a foreboding aura about it which does not abate when the librarian, in answer to a question, shoots out his finger and tells the hapless pilgrim to "look in the card catalog." Librarians here are encouraged to leave the desk, whenever possible, and stay with the patron until the desired information is found.

All of these tasks and programs are engaged in in an effort to make libraries as unforbidding and stimulating as possible. Many public libraries used to be grim places, indeed. Around here, with a flexible staff and cooperative teachers, we hope that they are less grim and more fun every year.

NOTE

1. Margaret A. Edwards, "The Public Library and Young Adults: A Viewpoint," in John Lubans, Jr., ed., Educating the Library User (New York: Bowker, 1974), p.56.

Appendix 1

THIRD GRADE TREASURE HUNT

Directions: Take pencil and paper with you. When you have written down all the words you find in the following places, they will make a sentence. Whisper the sentence to a librarian or teacher, and win your badge. Do not tell anyone else the sentence. If you don't finish during this period, you may come back any time this week after school and finish. (Leave the words where you find them.)

1. On the globe of the world in the children's department, find New Jersey.
2. Look up the book: Just So Stories in the card catalog.

3. Find the Just So Stories on the shelf, and look inside the front cover.
4. Look up "Indians of North America" in the index of the New Book of Knowledge.
5. Find the children's biography of Golda Meier, and look in the Table of Contents.
6. Look on page 13 of the book on palmistry.
7. Look in the June, 1976 issue of Cricket magazine. Find the article, "How to Become a Rock Hound."
8. Find the tape of Winnie the Pooh. Look inside the cover of the box.
9. Find the copying machine, and look in back of it.

If you can't find something, ask a teacher or librarian to help you.

Appendix 2

FIFTH GRADE MISSION IMPOSSIBLE

You will probably not be able to answer all the 35 questions that follow. Then again, you may astound us all. For the first 26 questions we want you to use the five underlined reference books. Most adults should know how to use those. The last 9 questions can be answered by using your head, looking around, or asking a librarian. We are here to help you. Don't be afraid to ask!

Who's Who in America 1980 or 1981
1. In what state was President Ronald Reagan born?
2. When was he governor of California?
3. What is Carol Burnett's address?
4. In what year was Reggie Jackson named the most valuable player in the American League?
5. What is the other name of Theodor Geisel?
Information Please Almanac 1980 or 1981
6. Who was President of the United States before Carter?
7. Which presidents are carved in Mt. Rushmore, in South Dakota?
8. What was the total population of the U.S. in 1970?
9. What are the last sixteen words of Lincoln's Gettysburg Address?
10. What is the distance in road mileage between New York and Washington, D.C.?
11. If you were born on March 3, 1968, what day of the week was that? (Look up "perpetual calendar.")
12. If you want to apply for a patent on your invention, to whom do you write?
Guinness Book of World Records 1980 or 1981
13. How long had the most overdue book ever returned to a library been kept out?

14. Who is the most successful songwriter of all time?
15. What is the world's record for nonstop talking?
16. What is the farthest recorded flight of a paper airplane?

Readers' Guide to Periodical Literature, v. 37

17. What issue of what magazine contains the first listed article about shyness?
18. In what issue of what magazine is there an article on the Beach Boys?
19. In what issue of what magazine is there an article on pennies?
20. In what issue of what magazine is the first listed article on the Loch Ness Monster?

Bartlett's Familiar Quotations, 14th or 15th ed.

21. Who said, "Home is the place where, when you have to go there, they have to take you in."?
22. Who said, "Three may keep a secret, if two of them are dead."?
23. Who said, "The great gray-green, greasy Limpopo River, all set about with fever trees."?
24. Who said, "Time for a little something."?
25. Who said, "A door is what a dog is perpetually on the wrong side of."?
26. Who said, "The only thing we have to fear is fear itself."?

General Questions

27. What are the Dewey decimal numbers for history?
28. In what year was Abraham Lincoln born?
29. What color was George Washington's white horse?
30. What evenings is the library open till 9 P.M.?
31. Who wrote 'Twas the Night before Christmas?
32. How much does it cost to make a copy in the copier?
33. What is the name of the Mayor of Ramsey?
34. What is playing at the Ramsey Cinema now?
35. What is the address of the Minolta Company in Ramsey?

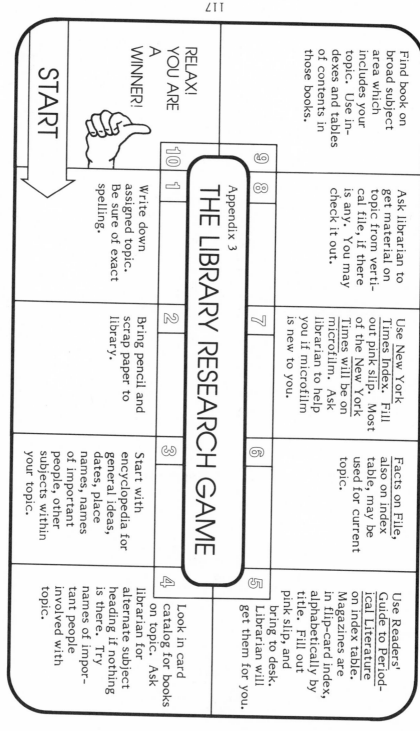

Appendix 3
THE LIBRARY RESEARCH GAME

START

RELAX! YOU ARE A WINNER!

Find book on broad subject area which includes your topic. Use indexes and tables of contents in those books.

Ask librarian to get material on topic from vertical file, if there is any. You may check it out.

Use New York Times Index. Fill out pink slip. Most of the New York Times will be on microfilm. Ask librarian to help you if microfilm is new to you.

Facts on File, also on index table, may be used for current topic.

Use Readers' Guide to Periodical Literature on index table. Magazines are in flip-card index, alphabetically by title. Fill out pink slip, and bring to desk. Librarian will get them for you.

Look in card catalog for books on topic. Ask librarian for alternate subject heading if nothing is there. Try names of important people involved with topic.

Start with encyclopedia for general ideas, dates, place names, names of important people, other subjects within your topic.

Bring pencil and scrap paper to library.

Write down assigned topic. Be sure of exact spelling.

10 1 8 9 7 6 5 4 3 2

sheffield
city
libraries

DAVID MILLER

All public libraries should welcome and accommodate visits by school classes at regular intervals so that the various services offered by the library can be brought to the attention of the children . . . . It is in the interests of the public librarian to encourage schools in this way since he thereby has access to 100% of the population in a particular age-group, an opportunity which will never again be offered to him once the children have left school.[1]

Most British public library authorities concur with this view, and many librarians have developed strong links with local schools to encourage them to use library facilities. Often, this results in class visits to the library, frequently to change books and sometimes to receive a little teaching on library use. This usually takes the form of a talk on the layout, discussion on the arrangement of books and perhaps a few simple games to practice finding a book or a subject. In fact, this is exactly how Sheffield City Libraries approaches user education for first and middle school children.[2]

However, because arrangements are left to the initiative of individuals, when teacher or librarian contact is broken the visits all too often cease. Sheffield City Libraries decided that this ad hoc arrangement was unsatisfactory for secondary children, and reached a virtually unique agreement with the city Education Department to approach the problem systematically. Every school child in the city, at least in theory, would be given the opportunity to visit the Central Library to look at the resources when 12 or 13 years old. This, of course, would be excellent publicity for the library but the objective was to be educational rather than just an outing. The value of the exercise was formally recognized by the funding arrangements. The salaries of the staff and cost of materials would be borne by the Education Department rather than Libraries budget. Even so, the staff would be appointed by the hierarchy of the Libraries Department and would be directly responsible to it. Only if further funding was needed, or if a dramatic change in the philosophy of the service was made, would the

Education Department be consulted. In fact, the service would be run on an agency basis, allowing even quite substantial changes to be made in the program without reference to the Education Department.

Surprisingly enough, this is not a recent innovation but dates back formally to 1942. Even as far back as 1924, the City Librarian, R. J. Gordon was recognizing in his annual report the value of introducing children to libraries.3 In that year 1,755 young people visited the library and "received instruction" although no record exists of its content. By the Second World War the work had become important enough to draw up the formal working arrangement, and in 1944 a full-time organizer was appointed. She was joined in 1958 by an assistant and that staffing situation still remains.4 By 1961, 6,000 children a year were visiting the Central Library.

The funding arrangements have always encouraged local schools to participate in the scheme, since it gave the instruction some credibility which it might not have otherwise had. However, despite this, English schools are largely autonomous; there can be no requirement on them to cooperate. They are annually invited, but are quite entitled to refuse to come or, more likely, ignore the invitation altogether. Two factors have contributed towards ensuring that a majority of schools do participate. First, the service has had a historical tradition of excellence, and second, library staff have persistently encouraged headteachers to send groups on visits. Only one comprehensive school out of the 39 in the city has yet to make use of the service.

BACKGROUND AND OBJECTIVES

A recent report suggests that there are three types of user education skills that children need:5

1. Library skills

These include most of the traditional library user education work such as using catalogs, library indexes, understanding Dewey, and knowing the layout of the library.

2. Study skills

Systematic rather than random information searching is involved here, that is, using contents and indexes in books and understanding how books are organized. Study skills also include using nonbook materials, having a thorough knowledge of library resources, knowing how to assess materials, detect bias and take effective notes.

3. Life skills

Information for life is a much wider category and crosses other subject barriers. It might include using telephone directories, street directories, learning how to fill in tax forms, and even simply finding a road on a map.

Clearly it would be impossible to cover all this ground in two hours, and the objectives of the school instruction service must be limited. It might also be said that many of the skills outlined are the responsibility of the teacher, or at least the school librarian rather than the public librarian. In fact, the service must be seen against a background of underdeveloped school resources centers with teachers having little knowledge of how to exploit the materials they do possess. Unfortunately, although the city recognizes the need for full-time librarians in every comprehensive school, some of which have 2,000 students, public expenditure cutbacks in Britain have meant that in practice the scheme has largely been frozen. School libraries are frequently run by teachers with varying degrees of enthusiasm, resources, and time and all too little skill. Inevitably user education is given correspondingly little thought, and is sometimes nonexistent. A recent survey of 26 Sheffield comprehensive school libraries revealed that only 6 had formal courses while 14 had not much more than a lesson a week reading a library book with perhaps a general introduction to the library.6 Six libraries had no instruction at all. Ironically, those schools which are most enthusiastic about school instruction tend to be those with the strongest resource centers and the best user education programs. The school which refuses to cooperate has one of the worst school libraries in the city.

Unfortunately, apathy about libraries among teachers is transmitted, no doubt unconsciously, to the children where it becomes disinterest, cynicism, or even hostility. The Central Library in Sheffield is a grand municipal building, distinctly forbidding to the average 12-year-old, and even some of our 37 branch libraries can be a little daunting. With all these factors in mind the objectives are now as follows:

1. To demonstrate to children that libraries can be interesting, even enjoyable and, above all, relevant.
2. To show what resources are available, preferably on subjects in which the children already have some interest.
3. To give them limited insight into how to use a library and how to use books thoughtfully.
4. To give them confidence in using the library.
5. To reassure the children that library staff can be helpful and interested in them.
6. To encourage them to join and use the library.

Some thought was given to the suitable age group to aim the instruction at; eventually, 12 years became recognized as most suitable. The children would be adult enough to assimilate information, but still impressionable. It would also prepare them for borrowing adult library books at 13. Experience has also shown that 13 is about the age when children begin to drift away from libraries to other interests. Repeat visits should be arranged throughout the student's school career as reinforcement, but only limited staff and resources are available, and there are about 6,000 to 7,000 individuals in the 12-13 age group in the city. In reality then, for many children the two hours spent in the Central Library is perhaps the only user education program they will ever receive. Inevitably the quality of the visit is all-important.

CONTENT OF VISIT

The visit is carefully planned to make it as balanced and varied as possible. Children (and adults) do not react well to being talked at for two hours, so it is important that they can relax for a part of the time, talk to their friends, and browse within the shelves. Practical work is an important element since children grasp difficult concepts better if they can experience systems in operation. The vital factor is the relationship that the librarian establishes with the children in the short time available. Their images of the staff can be changed radically by a little humor and some inquiries into their personal interests. A question and answer technique is always used to build up this relationship; it helps to assess the intellectual level of the children and ensures that all of them have grasped the concepts explained. As the average size of the class is approximately 25-30, it is convenient to split groups in two, each member of staff taking half. Each individual covers the same ground but in a different order. This puts less strain on public departments and catalogs and of course contributes towards a better working relationship. It is important that the tour is as visual as possible, so files of information, pictures, and examples are kept at strategic stopping places around the library.

Every tour begins with a general background talk on the library system, using a large map, showing pictures of district libraries that the children may be aware of. The funding of the service is discussed, and then the libraries of the central building are outlined, emphasizing the difference between lending and reference. Although it is not possible to take the children into the Reference Library for fear of disturbing readers, the main subjects covered by each section are described, highlighting leisure activities as well as academic and information sections. Examples of materials held are shown to the children.

A microfiche edition of a Los Angeles telephone directory is compared with the 15 hardback volumes for Zurich, to demonstrate the resources of the Business Library. Local history materials are always popular. The children enjoy seeing illustrations of familiar city streets as they looked one hundred years ago, and files of pictures and newspaper cuttings on their own school can even be produced.

A selection of books currently available in the Reference Library is kept in the classroom. These hundred or so books have been chosen to represent children's interests rather than for esoteric merit. After a brief introduction on the internal arrangement of books, each child attempts a question card on the book, with three questions graded in difficulty (see fig. 1). These are designed to ensure that the children have fully grasped the technique of using a reference book. Even at 12,

Guinness Book of Records 1981   032

1. Look at the picture at the top of page 200. How many eggs went into the largest omelette in the world?

2. Use the Index to find <u>Banana Eating Record</u>. How many bananas were eaten in 2 minutes?

3. Find <u>Sneezing</u>. How many days did Patricia Reay's sneezing fit last?

The Love of Soccer   796.334

1. Who is the former England Captain pictured at the top of page 36?

2. Use the Index to find <u>World Cup</u>. What is the full title of this competition?

3. Use the Contents to find <u>Soccer Chronology.</u> In which year did King Edward II ban the playing of soccer on the streets?

Fig. 1. Question Card on Reference Book

most are aware of the existence of a contents, index, and glossary in a book, but many do not really understand how to use them properly. This exercise also gives the children an opportunity to browse through books available in the library, and gives them an incentive to return. Popular books include Encyclopedia of Football, Horror Movies, and Health and Beauty. The situation is of course artificially created, but careful supervision at this stage means that errors in technique can be sifted out. Even so, the questions are composed so that the information obtained would still be of interest to any student of the subject. It is important to make it clear to the children why they are doing the exercise, so that they do not perceive it as a game in isolation.

The children then spend some time in the three lending libraries in the building, browsing around the Record and Children's libraries, and are given another practical exercise to do in the Central Lending Library. Until recently it was felt appropriate that the children use the dictionary catalog to find an individual book in the library using the author and title. However, after careful consideration it was decided that the 12-year-olds would benefit more from an attempt to find a subject, which would be more relevant to their immediate needs. Only the more intelligent of the children progress from this relatively simple task to the more difficult one of finding an individual "planted" title (see fig. 2).

All the papers are handed to the teacher at the end of the visit together with an answer key. This gives the teacher an opportunity to look through and mark the children's work, and to assess their progress in the skills used. Frequently teachers develop follow-up exercises to reinforce the concepts taught, although inevitably this depends on the initiative of the person concerned. The social value of the visit is also recognized by teachers, and essays can be written to highlight particular aspects.

The visit finishes with a tour of the basement stack of the building, a storage area for the reference titles. For most children this look behind the scenes is the highlight of the visit, an opportunity to see a quarter of a million books and periodicals in one sequence. Copies of old newspapers are kept available, including a number of famous events. The students are fascinated to read original reports of the Titanic sinking in 1912, the bombing of Sheffield in 1940, and the first men on the moon in 1969. Again, the newspapers are compared to microfilm editions and some children are even allowed to find the announcements of their births in the local newspaper.

Original archive material is also available, kept in storerooms with impressive safelike doors. Documents relating to life in Sheffield are produced, including a 1296 charter, a 1517 letter of Mary, Queen of Scots, and a school report from the nineteenth century. An account of the deaths of several school children with cholera in 1868 brings home to the children how life has changed in the city in the last 100 years.

At the end of the visit a leaflet is handed to each child to reinforce points made during the talks and all the children are encouraged to

SHEFFIELD CITY LIBRARIES
LIBRARY VISIT
Using the Catalog to Find a Subject

To find a subject in the catalog you must look at the <u>Blue Cards</u>.

1. (a) Find this subject and copy down the subject number on the dotted line:

Pigeon Keeping

see ....

   (b) Look for the books at this number.
   (c) Find this book: <u>Racing Pigeons</u> by <u>C. Osmon</u>.
   (d) What is the title of the chapter beginning on page 48?

2. (a) Write down the name of your favorite <u>interest,</u> <u>hobby</u> or <u>sport</u>.

   (b) Find the <u>Blue Card</u> for this subject.
   (c) Write the <u>subject number</u> here.

   (d) Find the books in the library and look at them.

3. Finding a Book
   <u>Your Book of Brasses</u> by <u>Malcolm Norris and Michael Kellett</u>
   (a) Find the <u>Orange Card</u> for this book.
   (b) Write the <u>subject number</u> here.

   (c) Find the book in the library.
   (d) What is the title of the chapter beginning on page 68?

Fig. 2. Subject Search

return to the library, to enroll and to ask the staff for any help they may need.

Inevitably, the ability levels of the classes vary enormously, and it is the responsibility of the library staff to assess the level of the group and adapt accordingly. In fact from experience, the visit can be changed significantly to suit any need. However, when some children find it difficult even to read and write, the content of the visit is invariably restricted considerably. Many children have a poor grasp of alphabet, and find it difficult to understand the intricacies of Dewey numbering. The language of books sometimes defeats them in their attempt to answer questions. Certainly, publishers have yet to realize that the arrangement within reference books leaves much to be desired if one is trying to find one small item of information.

ASSESSING ORGANIZATION

Traditionally the Libraries Department has relied on the Education Department to organize the service. The invitations are sent out by the latter and a rota is drawn up from the responses, each individual school giving its preferences for times and days. Recently this arrangement has become a little unsatisfactory since the person in the Education Department drawing up the timetable is not very responsive to particular needs, since she has no personal interest in the service. Teachers have complained that they are not receiving appropriate dates, or that invitations are not arriving. It is hoped that Libraries Department will take over responsibility for the administrative arrangements this year, so that schools can make more personal contact with the school instruction staff.

There are, of course, disadvantages to the children coming on a once only visit. The Central Library has many impressive resources, but it is easy to build the children's expectations to too high a level, which may be dashed at a later stage. Fellow librarians are not always as sympathetic to children as the section staff are, and need constant reminding of their importance in the general library structure. It is easy to give priority in a reference library to a businessman or local government official, rather than a 12-year-old whose immediate needs may not seem so vital. Those children may have their long-term views of the library flawed by a short encounter with an impatient or even hostile librarian. To some extent the school instruction staff play evangelistic roles with other library workers.

The library itself can be intimidating to socially disadvantaged groups and some children for all the efforts of the staff never seem to quite overcome the barriers. The visit is designed to inspire confidence in using libraries, but a small minority seem bewildered. However, the relationship built up with the children does help, and school instruction staff spend a proportion of their time campaigning for general improvements in library guiding and enquiry responses.

125

Relations with schools have always been something of a problem despite the persistence of the library staff. Ultimately we are dependent on the goodwill of individual teachers; often the personality of a headteacher will mean the difference between participation and non-participation. Probably Peter Stokes was overstating the case when he said that: "I shall argue that in reality libraries and schools are natural enemies, socially antagonistic."[7]

In context he felt that the objectives of schools to educate by feeding information to children, and those of libraries to allow free access to information required were in conflict. It certainly is fair to say that many teachers do not appreciate the value of libraries, resources, and especially user education itself. They perceive the visit as educational, but more like an outing to an ancient monument or fire station than an academic exercise. They frequently, in consequence, disappear to shop or to a nearby coffee-bar and await the end of the visit. Their involvement at a personal level would, and when given does, enhance the work considerably. Nobody expects every teacher to listen to almost identical talks repeatedly year after year, but many could adopt a more positive attitude towards the whole scheme. Groups could be better prepared for visits, and certainly more teachers could assist low-ability groups with practical work and help to ensure that they have truly grasped the skills outlined. It is never easy for one individual librarian to check all the work of a group of 15-20 children. Visits to schools to encourage teachers are considered an integral part of the service. Time spent in selling both the instruction scheme and libraries in general is rarely wasted; often it has sparked an internal school library user education program. To reinforce this, the section has produced a leaflet outlining the philosophy of the service, which is given to all teachers new to the school instruction scheme.

WORK WITH OLDER CHILDREN

It has been clear for some time that some kind of follow-up work was necessary to reinforce the service to 12-year-olds. However time has always been a prohibitory factor. The section has conducted 250 groups from that age group this year, and this leaves only a small number of vacancies for older children. It was decided that the age group most in need of user education above 12 was the 17-to-18-year-old group, students on the fringe of college and university. Consequently, work on a limited scale began recently, and now reaches almost fifty groups a year. From the beginning the tuition was on a suitably intensive level, designed to prepare the students for systematic information searching.

Handouts are extensively used, and the groups are introduced to materials they are usually not aware of. These include indexes and abstracts to periodicals, conference proceedings, theses, government publications, and sources of statistics. Usually the talk is tailored to the particular subject interest of the group, and examples shown are from that field. Photocopied pages are supplied to demonstrate layouts and the advantages and limitations of using the materials mentioned. By the end of each visit, the students are significantly better trained in methodical information retrieval.

PROGRAM RESULTS

Unfortunately, due to lack of resources no research is available to assess the value of the service. The individual reactions of the children are encouraging, nearly all leave having enjoyed their visit, and most tell us. Teacher feedback suggests that not only are the children excited by the visit, but also that they carry their enthusiasm into their own work and, best of all, their new-found skills are used in the school library to real benefit. Experience suggests that many enroll in the library as a result, although whether that use continues long-term is a debatable point. Certainly it can be said that most of the children do feel more confident in using the library, since many are seen returning on successive days.

THE FUTURE

The school instruction staff has always been conscious of the limitations of their program. Unfortunately, like most other public library authorities in Britain, Sheffield is carefully trimming its budget, and expansionary items are rarely considered. One area of particular concern to senior staff is the user instruction visits offered to adult education groups. Many such groups are conducted around the Central Library (circa 100 groups a year), but overall coordination of the visits is lacking. The standard of the instruction depends on the individual initiative of the librarian assigned to the group. Since the assignment is simply on a basis of a rota of librarians available, the quality of the visits varies enormously. It is particularly regrettable that no attempt is made to expand on any previous library user education given.

A recent staff review in the City Libraries has resulted in a suggestion that a new service be set up, probably entitled User Education, which would include the existing program for schools, a much improved adult education program, and even some staff training courses. It is hoped that an additional member of staff will be made available. However, it is probable that other professional staff will still have to be involved in user education. The main objectives of the idea are to improve the material used in programs, develop a coordinated strategy for user education, and sort out the booking system. It would also mean more variety for the school instruction staff.

Meanwhile, the work with the 12-year-olds continues to expand with teachers being regularly turned away because of lack of timetable space. It looks now as though a more suitable room may be created during the next year or so to house the visits, perhaps with facility for AV materials to replace the handmade ones now used.

Whatever changes are introduced, and those envisaged seem dramatic for a long-established section, the basic objectives are likely to remain the same. Preoccupied librarians must learn to share their interest in their materials with the children who visit. Many students, fascinated by their visit, respond with letters of thanks. The children write in their own inimitable ways:

". . . I had always wondered how the catalogue worked . . . ."

"Thank you for taking us around a wonderful library. . . ."

". . . the visit was helpful in teaching me how to use references and how to look up a book faster. . . ."

". . . not one bit of it was boring, I hope to come again. . . ."

"I got a card and went back to the library last Friday."

"I felt like a little librarian. . . ."

NOTES

1. Sheila G. Ray, Library Service to Schools, 2nd ed., Library Association Pamphlet no. 32 (London: Library Association, 1972), p.50.
2. The English educational system still varies from one local authority to another and is very complex indeed. However, Sheffield is slowly working towards five basic levels:

Nursery--Up to five years

First--Five years to eight years

Middle--Eight years to twelve years

Comprehensive--Twelve years to eighteen years (Secondary)

College/Polytechnic/University--Eighteen years onwards

3. Sheffield City Libraries, Annual report, 1923/24.
4. For a history of school instruction see:
Jennifer Jones, "Bringing to Books: An Outline of Public Library Instruction for Children, with Particular Reference to Sheffield City Libraries" (Master's thesis, Univ. of Sheffield, 1972), chaps. 3, 5.
5. Lancaster University, Centre for Educational Research and Development, Information Skills in the Secondary School, 1979.
6. Yvonne A. Lea, "User Education in Schools: A Survey of Methods Used in Comprehensive Schools in Sheffield" (Master's thesis, Univ. of Sheffield, 1977).
7. Peter Stokes, "Schools and Libraries--Ideologies in Conflict," Assistant Librarian 70, no. 9 (1977):134.

oakland
public
library

LEE WHITE

The Oakland Public Library has been experimenting for several years with ways to teach library research skills to the public. With fewer librarians and increased use of the library, the need to instruct the public becomes critical. Bibliographic resources have become both numerous and more complex. Library patrons need some study and experience to use sophisticated indexes. The necessary persistence to tackle formidable resources may depend upon the adequate attention and encouragement of a librarian. It has become almost impossible for the general public, on their own, to find substantial information on complex subjects. The time is gone when a librarian could spend a few minutes with a patron, explaining the Readers' Guide and suggesting several catalog entries, and feel satisfied that a subject would be covered credibly. That same subject may now be covered not only in Readers' Guide but in the Magazine Index, the Social Sciences Index, and other numerous resources.

For example, to locate a movie review, a patron must search in a variety of resources using a number of headings to find the necessary citations. The New York Times Film Reviews issues biennial compilations of film reviews printed in chronological order with access to specific reviews by title index. Film Review also utilizes a direct title index. Monthly Periodical Index uses the subject heading Motion Pictures-Reviews. The International Film Guide is not indexed but provides country by country essays on films released throughout the world which could require the patron to examine the entire U.S.A. entry to find a review. Periodical indexes such as Readers' Guide, Education Index, Social Sciences Index, Humanities Index, and Art Index all list movie review citations under the subject heading Motion Picture Reviews-Single Works and then the film title, a heading updated in 1977-78 from Moving Picture Plays-Criticisms, Plots, etc. Access and the Magazine Index both cite reviews under the title of the movie. The Music Index lists film reviews under the subject heading Films and Facts on File uses Motion Pictures-N.Y., Releases. Finding the right citations now requires more than a cursory sentence of explanation by the librarian. Even basic reference tools create confu-

129

sion since various indexes use different headings for what a patron considers the identical subject, and that subject not even given its real name--"movies."

For the Oakland Public Library, budget constraints have resulted in a reduction of personnel over the past five years. Today, the many demands on staff time often mean that the patron receives no more than minimal directions. Nevertheless, our librarians have to continue to guide the patron through the labyrinth of complicated materials, identify and acquire new resources, initiate computer searches, and understand the uses and limits of each resource. The Oakland Public Library maintains quality reference service in spite of a smaller staff and a leaner budget than in the past, but there is less librarian time to provide knowledgeable, consistent, and individualized help to patrons.

To address this public service problem, the Oakland Public Library designed a program to teach library patrons to use reference tools independently. In seeking a model for instruction of the public in library resources, the staff searched the library literature and visited other institutions. We found that other public libraries most often use booklists and library tours to introduce library materials and their locations. Such lists generally avoid tools which are specialized, difficult to use, or fail to generate interest in reference works or even clearly explain their purpose. Tours of the library are useful, but are usually restricted to an overview of a subject department and do not provide hands-on experience with reference materials.

After some experimentation and realization that the usual lists and tours provide a very limited exposure to the great variety of bibliographic resources, the Oakland Public Library decided to offer library instruction classes patterned on a course taught at the University of California, School of Library and Information Studies. The course at the Berkeley campus, Bibliography I, teaches the use of the University Library System to undergraduate students. The course has been growing in popularity for a decade and its record of success is well established. Careful thought was given to adapting the format of Bibliography I to the resources of a sizable public library (Oakland Public Library has some 800,000 volumes) and to the intended audience of non-student adult library patrons. After reviewing several teaching sources, we decided to use the revised edition of the Berkeley text, Methods of Library Use: Handbook for Bibliography I by B. Johnson, E. Sibley, and P. Wallman (Berkeley: University of California, 1979) because of its emphasis on search strategy. Oakland Public Library has offered two successful series of classes using Bibliography I as a model. In 1978, the first series of classes generated considerable public interest, proving feasibility of such instruction for the public. Two Oakland Public Library programs offered to adults have used similar approaches and formats. The common aims were: (1) to teach serious library users reusable skills of lasting value by use of a search strategy motif; (2) to alleviate the problems caused by staff shortages which hinder complete in-depth reference service; and (3) to promote public awareness of the library's resources. Search strategy, as used in many library teaching programs as well as our own, attempts to organize seemingly disjointed information sources into a general pattern that can be followed by users and to teach this pattern to users for their own application. While the user's questions will vary over time and from library to library, the approach will not change. Search strategy suggests the inquiry process be taken in a series of steps:

1. Background reading to gain an appreciation of the breadth and span of a topic. General encyclopedias are usually of value in summarizing what are often broad topics.

2. Narrowing or restating the topic in specific terms may involve general and subject encyclopedias and dictionaries. This is often the step where a tentative statement is developed for an appropriate topic.

3. Deciding to use books (using the author/title or subject catalog) or periodicals (using the general and subject periodical indexes) depends on the depth and currency of the topic. An item discovered in the narrowing-down phase, for example, in an encyclopedia's bibliography, may serve as the initial entry into the card catalog. Subsequently, the card catalog tracing may provide alternative subject access to other materials in the library.

4. Using other sources of information, as appropriate, such as government reports and nonbook media through the special indexes available.

The Oakland course centers around the student's own project. The choice of research subject is of prime importance and the librarian must give considerable guidance to the student in establishing the scope of the topic. The most satisfactory subjects are those which cross several disciplines and introduce the student to a wide variety of resources. For example, the subject of jade may be pursued through folklore, mythology, geology, art, history, archeology, and jewelry. Esoteric or especially hard-to-find information is challenging, but it is also discouraging to new students and should be avoided unless the student has an unusual interest. Likewise, if the subject is very current and will be found mostly in periodicals and newspapers and their indexes, the learning experience will be limited. Above all, the subjects chosen should be capable of sustaining the interest of the student over the term of the project. Water polo, for example, will be covered quickly without exposure to many resources. Choosing a new topic at each session also tends to disrupt the student's understanding of the information network. The subjects are agreed upon during the first class session and more participants sustain interest in the project during the course if their subject is well chosen. Some students will be satisfied with fewer classes if, for example, they learn more quickly or choose a less complex subject for their project. When the subject is agreed upon, it can be developed into the student's specific topic and the search strategy can be planned.

The course format that Oakland Public Library chose is a series of six two-hour sessions. Each session is loosely divided into three segments; the meetings begin with a talk by the librarian on a standard library tool such as subject headings, the card catalog or periodical indexes. The students and the librarian next move into the library and work with the tool under discussion, using a "work sheet" provided. Students will use their own subjects for each project. The librarian gives individual help during this time. The final segment of the class session is spent discussing the problems and discoveries encountered by the students. This final wrap-up period is very important, as students summarize and record their own progress and also learn about the resources and search techniques, successful and otherwise, used by others in the group.

The intent in Oakland has been to address nonstudent adults, although students were not excluded and each group included some adults in college. Sessions varied from three to ten people with an average of six. Because the two series of classes offered thus far have been an experiment for Oakland, the courses were not formally advertised.

Librarians alerted patrons who showed interest and several signs in the library announced the course with the lead-in "Do you need help with research in the Library?" One course was scheduled for Saturday mornings and the other series was held on Wednesday evenings. Some students were satisfied in two or three weeks, but others finished the six weeks and seemingly would have continued indefinitely.

As students completed the class, some showed interest in doing more advanced research on their own. One pilot project was prepared for an advanced study unit under the National Endowment Planning Grant. A subject was chosen from several presented by students and a sample unit was designed on the topic "Black American Women Poets." This unit included a slide/tape presentation on appropriate resources and their use.

The same basic six-week program described here was implemented in the Summer and Fall of 1981 through a grant to the Oakland Public Library to work jointly with the Oakland Public Schools. This Library Services Construction Act Grant, awarded through the California State Library, taught library use skills using both the school libraries and the public library resources for student credit.

The bibliography class was held in two five-week sessions for which high school students moving into their senior year received credit. The course was designed for the students to do independent bibliographic research using general tools and search techniques in the Oakland Public Library. In the first session, students were allowed to choose their own subject, but even with teacher's approval, many topics were too broad, inappropriate, or not well covered in the Oakland Public Library collections. Five weeks was not enough time to revise an inappropriate topic and do satisfactory research. For the second session, a list of topics covering a wide range of varied topics was developed by the Oakland Public Library's Main Library staff and checked for information available in our collection.

The Main Library staff was briefed on work that students would be doing and given guidelines on the amount of help to give to students. Contact between the students and librarians was vital to the students' understanding of the librarian's role and to use of the source materials. An additional factor was the students' sharing their experiences by participation in class discussions. Problems and successes were analyzed so that all students benefited from each other's work.

Class assignments on the source materials emphasized effective use rather than correct answers. General class discussions worked well and students contributed to each other's projects.

The resulting bibliographies were very individual projects; the weaknesses and strengths of each student's work were apparent in choice of materials and in annotations.

A further project involved a high school where the school librarian and the teachers felt library instruction, although not part of the standard school curricula, was important. Each teacher included some time for the Oakland Public Library to give library instruction in a subject course so that 100 students received "a first step to making many students aware of their libraries and interested in learning about them and utilizing libraries." (LSCA Application, p. A-13-4) This type of cooperation developed high interest in library research for both students and teachers.

The search strategy is, in itself, the primary message. The course is not on studying the content of information on selected subjects but on finding and retrieving the information. Although the class is concerned with the process of finding information, the content is of most interest to the student; therefore, how to judge the resource is also discussed and criteria such as currency, credibility, and authenticity are considered. Students plan their research strategy in advance and consider and adapt it as the project progresses. Each student keeps a log or diary of research efforts. It clarifies and emphasizes the search process, suggests a pattern of bibliographic organization, and organizes notes taken during a search. The instructor can use the log as a basis for recommending further search strategy. It is also helpful for the student to compile a bibliography on the chosen subject; a tangible product is very rewarding.

In our attempts to inculcate the search strategy concept we have found that formal lectures and "show and tell" use of reference books are nonproductive. Handout sheets and an overhead projector with good transparencies are useful. With some thought the instructor can develop learning exercises that interest and benefit everyone. For example, "reverse indexing" is always a challenge: the student reads an article in an older issue of Time or Newsweek, decides on its subject heading, and then tries to find it in an index. This exercise usually brings instant understanding of the need for both consistency and flexibility in subject heading terminology.

To further emphasize the search strategy concept we stress that much important information is not in the catalog. The students are delighted to discover the special files that seem to grow around every reference desk--a recipe index, a file of most-often-asked reference questions, or a list of local authors. The range of periodicals, documents, pamphlets, and nonprint resources is usually an exciting surprise to our students, even those with years of confident library use.

Second, the librarian as a trained information specialist who can assist and guide a patron through the complexities of reference and research is emphasized. The success of the course depends on the use of a librarian as teacher and on the librarian's reference skills. The support and cooperation of the entire staff is, of course, also of vital importance.

The librarian as an instructor reinforces the role of information provider. The usual teaching requirements of relating well to the students and enjoying teaching are basic. Beyond that, the librarian must have a clear understanding of the structure and function of the public library and possess broad knowledge of reference work. Besides assisting students during the class meetings, the librarian spends preparation time reviewing possible sources for each student's subject, anticipating the questions and problems likely to arise. Initially, to design and implement the course seems formidable and is time-consuming. However, there are many good teaching resources available and the essential requirements remain--the skills and practices used daily by all reference librarians. Once the course is organized, the lesson plans and materials may be used for future courses with only minor revisions and updating.

Third, we emphasize that library research skills are transferable. As students learn to search one subject and discover organized information structures, they are reminded that these same structures exist in other areas of interest. This often comes as a surprise and immediately inspires more confidence in the somewhat Byzantine bibliographic world. Learning how to find information efficiently saves time and avoids frustration, whether for career, education, or recreational concerns.

Fourth, the course embraces a philosophy of organized knowledge. The public library is a massive and invaluable resource, yet the important thing is not the library itself, but the knowledge it holds. Likewise, call numbers, catalogs, indexes, and interlibrary loan are only means to an end. Utilizing these means is less intimidating when the patron understands that their purpose is to produce the information. A picture of the patterns and networks of information organization is new and illuminating to the student. People are delighted and intrigued as they come to realize that no matter what the question, the answer is almost always in the library.

ASSESSMENT

The benefits students derive from the course are the skills they learn and can use for the rest of their lives. The success they experience through their progress is obvious to them. No tests, grades, or requirements are asked--we rely on the students' own motivation.

The public library can reaffirm its roots as a "public university" by emphasizing continuing self-education, as well as "beginning" education. From the early days, the public library has been a place where everyone could learn, new immigrants and the under-educated as well as the constant reader. Today, public libraries often design and plan continuing education programs that are paid for by community colleges. Programs such as genealogy classes, local history courses, and book and film review groups have been part of Oakland's services for some time. The patron who cannot or chooses not to participate in these formal classes continuously uses the library for independent learning.

A class on use of library resources also serves as a means to increase the patron's general awareness of the whole public library. The students who attended our classes were exposed to many other programs of the library: children's services, courses held in other branches, and services to special groups. Classes also provide the librarian with insights about user images of the library and their expectations. This informal user input can help the library to be more effective, as the students' remarks often convey nebulous "gut feelings" which are not satisfactorily identified by formal survey techniques. Increased familiarity with the library's resources offers the additional benefit of diminishing the library's institutional image in the public's eye. These points were clearly expressed in our student evaluation sheets at the end of courses.

Satisfied, loyal consumers go a long way to ensure the success of a product. Likewise, library users who are involved and enlightened through participation in the library research classes form an influential group of library advocates. The testimony of some participants has been more effective than formal publicity in support of the library services. Their specific knowledge of the library, expressed in a public forum, clearly reinforces the position of the library as a vital public service justifying strong financial support.

Appendix 1

ENCYCLOPEDIAS WORKSHEET

An encyclopedia can give you a clear understanding of your topic by providing a definition of your subject and background information.

GENERAL ENCYCLOPEDIAS SEARCH

Consult three encyclopedias: The Encyclopedia Americana, Encyclopaedia Britannica and Collier's Encyclopedia. Look up your topic directly and in the index volume if the set of encyclopedias has one. List the subject headings which discuss your topic, locate the articles in the encyclopedia that you found in the index, and examine the encyclopedia articles and select one from each encyclopedia that covers your topic well. Compare the three articles for the following qualities:

What is the length of the article (number of paragraphs or pages)?

Does the article have clear illustrations, photographs, or maps?

Is the article easy to understand?

Are there references to related articles elsewhere in the encyclopedia?

Is there a list of suggested additional readings, books, or articles?

Is the article up-to-date and can you tell who wrote it?

Choose the encyclopedia article that seems the most useful to your topic and make a correct and complete listing for it so that it can be found again easily.

SUBJECT ENCYCLOPEDIAS SEARCH

Look up your topic in the index of one suitable subject encyclopedia such as:

Science: The McGraw-Hill Encyclopedia of Science and Technology

Social Science: The International Encyclopedia of the Social Sciences

Art: Encyclopedia of World Art

Music: Grove's Dictionary of Music and Musicians

U.S. History: Dictionary of American History

Literature: Cassell's Encyclopedia of World Literature

How do the articles in these subject encyclopedias differ from the general encyclopedias? Are they more detailed, longer, more technical, or have better book lists?

Which encyclopedia do you think is the best for your subject? Make a correct and complete listing for it so that it can be found again.

Appendix 2

CARD CATALOG WORKSHEET

The card catalog is a guide to books and documents about your topic that are available in the library. For most books (and other materials)

bought for the public's use, several cards are filed in the card catalog. For each item, the author's name, the book title, and one or more subject headings are filed alphabetically.

CARD CATALOG SEARCH

During this exercise, a listing will be made of all possible subject headings under which you might find information on your topic.

Make a list of words that best describe your topic. Look up these words in the <u>Library of Congress List of Subject Headings</u> and the <u>Sears List of Subject Headings</u>. List the subject headings you find and any Dewey decimal numbers shown with them. Look up all your subject headings in the card catalog.

Does the catalog use the same subject headings you listed?

Does the catalog use the subject headings you found in Sears or in the LC Subject Headings?

Does the catalog refer you by "see" or "see also" directions to other subject headings?

Choose a series of books listed on the subject cards in the catalog that seem to cover your subject. There may be additional subject headings shown on the bottom of the card (tracings). Add any new subject headings to your list.

Look at your series of books listed on subject cards again and write down the Dewey decimal numbers shown on the upper left corner of the cards.

Take your list of Dewey numbers and locate them on the library's reference book shelves. Examine the books that show your Dewey numbers and list the numbers that seem the best sources of information for your subject.

How many reference books did you find on your topic?

How many Dewey numbers did you examine to locate these books?

Which Dewey number seems the most useful to your topic?

Choose the one reference book that seems to contain the most useful information on your topic. Make a correct and complete listing of this book with a few sentences about why it seemed the most useful to your topic.

bibliography

The items listed below have been suggested by the contributors and others, and include those that I've come across while putting this book together. Two particularly good sources, covering more than just public libraries, have been Deborah Lockwood's annotated Library Instruction: A Bibliography (Westport, Conn.: Greenwood, 1979) and the annual annotated bibliographies edited by Hannelore B. Rader and published by LOEX.

" 'Alivebrary' for Students." American Libraries 12 (1981):44. Includes a four-page insert for primary and secondary school students and their teachers for fun tours of the library. Age 4 up.

Anspaugh, Sheryl. "Public Libraries: Teaching the User?" In Progress in Educating the Library User, edited by John Lubans, Jr., pp.125-32. New York: Bowker, 1978.

Berry, John. "Editorial: 'Pilgrim's Progress' and 'The Bible.' " Library Journal 115 (1981):831. Calls for a national-level agency to develop a "crash program" of library instruction to reach all Americans from kindergarten onward.

Birren, J. The Psychology of Aging. Englewood Cliffs, N.J.: Prentice-Hall, 1964.

Boehm, Eric H. "On the Second Knowledge: A Manifesto for the Humanities." Libri 22 (1972):312-23.

Broadus, Robert N., ed. The Role of the Humanities in the Public Library. Chicago: American Library Assn., 1979.

Brooks, Jean. "User Education in Public Libraries." In Seminar on User Education Activities: The State of the Art in Texas, pp.19-23. Houston: Texas Library Assn., 1977. ED 138 247. Surveys 47 public libraries.

Childers, Thomas. The Effectiveness of Information Service in Public Libraries: Suffolk County: Final Report. Philadelphia: Drexel Univ., School of Library and Information Science, 1978.

Dale, Sheila M. "The Adult Independent Learning Project: Work with Adult Self-Directed Learners in Public Libraries." Journal of Librarianship 11 (1979):83-106.

————. "Another Way Forward for Adult Learners: The Public Library and Independent Study." Studies in Adult Education 12 (April 1980):29-38.

DeRivera, Joseph, comp. Field Theory as Human Science. New York: Gardner, 1976.

DeSomogyi, Aileen. "Library Skills: Now or Never." School Library Journal 22(1975):37.

Doyle, Carol M. "Media for Library Skills Instruction." Previews 7 (February 1979):2-8.

"Educating Librarians and Users for a New Model of Library Service." Two audiotapes of a program given at the American Library Association Annual Conference, July 1, 1975, San Francisco. Los Angeles: Development Digest, 1975.

Edwards, Margaret A. "The Public Library and Young Adults: A Viewpoint." In Educating the Library User, edited by John Lubans, Jr., pp.56-58. New York: Bowker, 1974.

Eyster, George W. Institute Series for Developing Public Library Services for Disadvantaged Adults. Volume 2, Annual Report for 1974. Morehead, Ky.: Appalachian Adult Education Center, Morehead State Univ., 1975. ED 111 413.

Fiction Friction. 16mm, 18 min. 1973. Cellar Door Cinema, Drawer P, Osterville, Mass.

Frazier, Patrick. "Alien in the Reading Room." American Libraries 11 (1980):536-39. Mentions Library of Congress's guidance concept for orientation of users.

Freire, P. Pedagogy of the Oppressed. New York: Seabury, 1970.

Frey, Amy L., and Saul Spiegel. "Educating Adult Users in the Public Library." Library Journal 104 (1979):894-96.

Gant, Donna. "Richmond's Open High School Opens Windows on the Library." Virginia Librarian 20 (July 1974):8-9.

Goggin, Margaret, et al. The Report on the Instruction in the Use of Libraries in Colorado Presented to the Colorado Council on Library Development by (Its) Committee on Instruction in the Use of Libraries. Denver, Colo.: The Committee, 1973. Of note for its analysis of all types of libraries; including a 20-page analysis of public libraries by Alma Sheff based on 68 returned questionnaires.

Hannigan, Margaret C. "Orientation of the Out-of-School Adult to the Use of Public Libraries." ALA Bulletin 61 (1967):829-30.

Hendley, Margaret. "The Librarian as Teacher: Research Skills for Library Patrons at Kitchener Public Library." Ontario Library Review 63 (1979):45-48.

Hiemstra, R. The Older Adult and Learning. Lincoln, Neb.: Department of Adult and Continuing Education, Univ. of Nebraska, 1975.

Hoegh, Gloria, and Sharon Lenz. "A Mixed Bag Teaches Users: Oshkosh Public Library Uses Traditional and Novel Means." Wisconsin Library Bulletin 73 (1977):165-66.

Holmes County School District. On-site Library Training Program for School and Community in an Economically and Culturally Deprived County. Lexington, Mass.: The District, 1979. ED 183 162.

Houle, Cyril O. The Inquiring Mind. Madison: Univ. of Wisconsin Pr., 1961.

Hunter, Carman St. John, and David Harman. Adult Illiteracy in the United States: A Report to the Ford Foundation. New York: McGraw-Hill, 1979.

Hyland, Anne. "Profile of Library Skills in Ohio." Ohio Media Spectrum 31 (1979):12-17.

Irving, Ann. "New Directions for Libraries." Library Association Record 81 (1979):179ff.

———. Partnerships: Libraries, Open Learning and Adult Education. Mimeographed. Loughborough, England: Loughborough Univ. of Technology, 1979.

Jeffrey, Penelope S. "Library Instruction for Young Adults in Public Libraries." In Educating the Library User, edited by John Lubans, Jr., pp.53-55. New York: Bowker, 1974.

Johnstone, J. Volunteers for Learning. Hawthorne, N.Y.: Aldine, 1965.

Kidd, J. How Adults Learn. New York: Association Pr., 1973.

Knox, A. Adult Development and Learning. San Francisco: Jossey-Bass, 1977.

Leopold, Carolyn Clugston. School Libraries Worth Their Keep. Metuchen, N.J.: Scarecrow, 1972. While stressing school libraries, this work offers many relevant ideas to the public librarian.

Let's Learn. 16mm. 1979. Ramapo Catskill Library System, 619 North St., Middletown, N.Y.

Lewsey, Elizabeth. "Complaints from a Librarian." Art and Craft in Education 253 (February 1979):3.

Library and Information Service Needs of the Nation: Proceedings of a Conference on the Needs of Occupational, Ethnic, and Other Groups in the United States. Washington, D.C.: National Commission on Libraries and Information Science, 1974. Features chapters such as "Women, Homemakers and Parents," "Young Children," "Young Adults and Students," "Aging Americans," etc.

"Library Course Scores with Vegas Teenagers." American Libraries 8 (October 1977):509.

Lubans, John, Jr., ed. Educating the Library User. New York: Bowker, 1974.

———. "Library Literacy" (a column on user education). RQ 19 (1980):325-28. This is the first of the quarterly columns on instruction in use in all types of libraries.

Lynch, Mary Jo. "Reference Interviews in Public Libraries." Library Quarterly 48 (1978):119-42.

Martin, Lowell A. Students and the Pratt Library: Challenge and Opportunity. Deiches Fund Studies of Public Library Service, no.1. Baltimore, Md.: Enoch Pratt Free Library, 1963.

Maslow, A. Religions, Values and Peak Experiences. New York: Penguin, 1976.

———. Toward a Psychology of Being. 2nd ed. New York: Van Nostrand, 1968.

Michener, James A. "How to Use a Library." Two-page advertisement for the International Paper Company. Psychology Today 14 (October 1980):61-62.

Molz, Kathleen R. "The 'State of the Art' of Public Library Orientation." Maryland Libraries 34 (Winter 1968):10-17.

"National Library Week Theme Promotes Library Call Numbers." American Libraries 12 (1981):41. Report on NLW material that includes brochure on how to use the library.

Newman, Ruth T. "Instructing the Out of School Adult in Public Library Use." In Educating the Library User, edited by John Lubans, Jr., pp.59-68. New York: Bowker, 1974.

Nordling, Jo Anne. Dear Faculty. Framingham, Mass.: Faxon, 1976. Chapter 11, pp.150-53, discusses an "expedition to the Public Library."

Olson, Edwin E. Survey of User Service Policies in Indiana Libraries and Information Centers. Indiana Library Studies, no.10. Bloomington, Ind.: n. p., 1970. Survey of "user instruction and educational programs" in public libraries.

Paltridge, Cynthia. "Educating Children in Library Use." In Proceedings, Adelaide, 1969, pp.454-59. Sidney, Australia: Library Assn. of Australia, 1971.

Pate, Judy. "Public Library Response: The Present." In Passages: Library Instruction for Lifelong Enrichment: 1978 Conference Proceedings, pp.15-18. Lexington, Va.: Virginia Library Assn., 1979.

Penland, P. "Self-initiated Learning." In Adult Education 23 (1979):170-79.

Penn, Phyllis. "Children Learn Library Use." Wisconsin Library Bulletin 75 (1979):55-56.

Prince, William, and Charles Bownson, eds. Passages: Library Instruction for Lifelong Enrichment: Proceedings of the VLA Library Instruction Forum Preconference, November 29-30, 1978. Richmond, Va.: Virginia Library Assn., 1979.

"Quadrus Promotes Libraries for Inner-City Children." American Libraries 12 (1981):46. Comic book portrays research paper steps. Results: registration doubled; circulation up 5 percent; professional services up 32 percent.

Rawles, Beverly. Group Library Tours for Disadvantaged Adults. Public Library Training Institutes Library Service Guide, no.13. Morehead, Ky.: Appalachian Adult Education Center, Morehead State Univ., 1975. ED 108 651.

Reenstjerna, Fred R. "Standards Committee; Report on Survey 1: Librarians." LIFLINE Newssheet, no.15 (1980):6-9. Survey of Virginia libraries on user education.

Rishøj, Jørgen. "Library Guidance for the Public and Library PR as Seen from Bibliotekscentralen." Scandinavian Public Library Quarterly 10 (1977):46-51.

Rogers, C. Freedom to Learn: A View of What Education Might Become. New York: Merrill, 1964.

Scarpellino, Ann. "School-Public Library Cooperation: Some Practical Approaches." Unabashed Librarian 32 (1978):29-30.

"Schoolteachers Get Library's 10 Laws for Good Research." Plainspeaking 1 (1977):3. Adapted from The Unabashed Librarian, no.22.

Shelton, John L. "Project Uplift: Cultivating the Library Habit." Wilson Library Bulletin 50 (September 1975):59-62.

Smith, Frank. "Public Library Response: The Past." In Passages: Library Instruction for Lifelong Enrichment: 1978 Conference Proceedings, pp.13-14. Lexington, Va.: Virginia Library Assn., 1979.

Solon, Avis, and Lare Mischo. "Ways through the Library Maze: For Public Library Users in Search of Service." Wisconsin Library Bulletin 73 (1977):163-64.

Stibitz, Mildred T. "Library Workshop for Adults." ALA Bulletin 60 (1966):937-41.

"Suffolk County Library." Infuse 4 (June 1980):6-9. Description of a public library user education course.

Tarakan, Sheldon Lewis. "Opening the Attic Door: Bibliographic (and Other) Instruction at the Port Washington Public Library." Bookmark 38 (Fall 1979):249-52.

Tough, A. The Adult's Learning Projects. 2nd ed. Toronto, Ontario: Institute for Studies in Education, 1979.

"User Education in Public Libraries . . ." Infuse 3 (June 1979):4. Description of a conference on the subject held at Loughborough, England.

Volker, Paul. The Spacey Adventures of Platopunk. Columbus, Ohio: Public Library of Columbus and Franklin County, 1979. An 8-page comic strip.

"White House Conference, U.S.A." Infuse 4 (April 1980):5-7. Reprint of resolutions important to user education.

Whiting, B. C. "Introducing Children to the Library." Assistant Librarian 64 (February 1971):26.

Winslow, Theresa. "Homework Helpers." New Jersey Libraries 12 (September 1979):16-17.

Zahorski, Marijean A. "Programs Can Instruct." Wisconsin Library Bulletin 75 (1979):53-54.

contributors

SHEILA DALE

Sheila Dale is a graduate of London University and an Associate of the Library Association. As Chief Liaison Librarian at the Open University Library, she leads a team providing special services to academic staff and has been instrumental in developing a program of user education for students. Previously she taught in France, and worked in public libraries and college of education libraries, where her final appointment was as a tutor-librarian. Convinced of the educational potential of libraries, in 1978 she visited the United States on a Churchill Fellowship to study the Adult Independent Learning Project, with a view toward its possible application in Great Britain.

MARGARET HENDLEY

Margaret Hendley is Coordinator of Information Services, Kitchener Public Library in Kitchener, Ontario. She received her M.L.S. from the School of Library and Information Service, University of Western Ontario in 1970, followed by postgraduate work at the School of Library, Archive and Information Studies, University College, London, England in 1976. Margaret has published in the Canadian Library Journal and the Ontario Library Review. She spoke at the CLA 1981 conference in Hamilton, Ontario on the topic "Library Instruction in the 1980s."

ANNE M. HYLAND

Anne M. Hyland is the Director of Curriculum and Instruction for the Northeastern Local School District, Springfield, Ohio, and former State Supervisor, School Media Programs with Ohio Department of Education. She has served on the Board of Directors of the Ohio Educational Library Media Association for six years, and is the editor of Ohio Media Spectrum. Dr. Hyland's doctorate is from the University of Toledo in Curriculum and Instruction. She has been a featured speaker at numerous presentations and is the author of The Ohio School Library Media Test.

JOHN LUBANS, JR.

John Lubans, Jr., has been active in public services librarianship as a researcher, author, speaker, and practitioner. Among his publications are two which he edited: Educating the Library User (1974) and Progress in Educating the Library User (1978). While Assistant Director for Public Services at the University of Colorado (1970-78) he directed and evaluated the National Endowment for the Humanities (NEH) Council on Library Resources program there. In the American Library Association he has served on the Instruction in the Use of Libraries Committee and the 800-member Library Instruction Round Table, most recently (1981) as program chairperson. Currently he is Assistant University Librarian for Public Services at Duke University; a consultant for reader services librarianship and program evaluation; and the editor of the "Library Literacy" column in RQ.

DAVID MILLER

David Miller holds a master's degree from the Sheffield Postgraduate School of Librarianship. His professional work began in 1975 at the London Borough of Barnet Library. Since 1979 he has been School Instruction Librarian for the Sheffield City Libraries. He is a frequent guest speaker at library schools and professional conferences.

ILENE NELSON

Ilene Nelson is one of the select few who can claim Laramie, Wyoming as a birthplace. Her library career began as a student assistant in her high-school library. After receiving the M.S.L.S. from the University of Kentucky she was appointed to the University of South Carolina Library where she was involved in user education research for several years. For three-and-a-half years she was a reference librarian at the Spartanburg County Public Library. In August 1981, she returned to campus at the Duke University Library. Ms. Nelson is an active member of the North Carolina Library Association and the ALA Library Instruction Round Table (LIRT), speaking at the founding conference and at its meeting in the summer of 1981 in San Francisco.

JUDY PATE

Judy Pate received a B.A. in history from Meredith College and a M.A. in education from East Carolina University. Since 1976 she has worked as a reference librarian for the Virginia Beach Public Library. Earlier she worked as a reference librarian for the East Carolina University Library. She is a member of the Virginia Library Association and its Library Instruction Forum. She has participated as a workshop leader and speaker on library instruction at various regional and statewide conferences.

ANN SCARPELLINO

Ann Scarpellino has been Young People's Librarian at the Ramsey Free Library in Ramsey, New Jersey since 1973. She received her B.A. from Smith College in 1955, and, along with a number of other "retreads" (returning middle-aged women), her M.L.S. from Columbia University in 1973. She is a former teacher.

JOHN C. SHIRK

By practical definition a "high school dropout," John Shirk went on to pursue three careers, navy yeoman, United Methodist minister, and public library librarian. Chance, good fortune, and the G.I. Bill paved the way for him to become a lifelong learner. He received his M.S.L.S. from Syracuse and was the recipient of a Mott Fellowship to attend Texas A&M University where he is completing an advanced degree in Educational Administration with a minor in Adult Education. He was a public librarian for seven years with the Houston Public Library.

FRANK SMITH

Frank Smith has worked as a reference librarian for the Virginia Beach Public Library since 1975. Before that he served as reference librarian at Radford College. He received an A.B. degree in sociology from the College of William and Mary and a M.S.L.S. from the University of Kentucky. He is a member of the Virginia Library Association and its Library Instruction Forum. He has participated as a workshop leader and speaker on library instruction at various regional and statewide conferences.

PEGGY SULLIVAN

Peggy Sullivan, at the time this book was written, was the Assistant Commissioner for Extension Services at Chicago Public Library. Before that she was on the faculty of the University of Chicago Graduate Library School. Currently she is the Dean of the College of Professional Studies at Northern Illinois University. She is well known to the profession here and abroad for her publications and most recently for her creative and vibrant presidency of the American Library Association.

LEE WHITE

Lelia White earned her Bachelor and M.L.S. degrees from the University of California at Berkeley, and taught Bibliography I (the noted library skills class) at that campus. She has worked in public libraries as a reference librarian, branch librarian and supervising librarian, and has served as Director of Library Services at the Oakland Public Library since 1976. She is a member of the California Library Association, Urban Libraries Council, American Library Association, Public Library Association, and the California Institute of Libraries.